It's Not Just Black or White

To John
From Warren Ricky Brown

Hope you enjoy the book.
Richard Aubry

Thank you for your support
"It's not about Black or White"
Edd "Carew" White

It's Not Just Black or White

Richard Aubry, Ed.D. and Warren "Ricky" Brown

ISBN-13: 9781523608201
ISBN-10: 152360820X
Library of Congress Control Number: 2016905783
CreateSpace Independent Publishing Platform
North Charleston, South Carolina

Contents

Acknowledgements

⁓

WRITING A BOOK CAN BE a tedious and challenging enterprise for the author and those close to him. In this endeavor, I'd like to especially give thanks to my wife, Mo, and to Ricky Brown, my co-author and co- captain of the Farmville All-Stars. My wife continually suggested I write the story of my time with the All-Stars baseball team. We discussed that three-year span in the mid-1970s numerous times. Mo would cajole me to write the story of those times that seemed so poignant. After hearing of the passing of Carl Robinson, one of my former teammates, I decided I couldn't wait any longer to share my story of the Farmville All-Stars. Mo was extremely helpful during the manuscript writing, offering suggestions and ideas. Her technical support was critical to the process, as I continue to be technology challenged.

I must profusely thank Ricky Brown for all his efforts in the planning phase of this book. Ricky was instrumental in contacting former players, arranging for space for interviews to be conducted, and discussing with me events of the past years involving the All-Stars. This book could not have been written without his support. He was an avid contributor and a wonderful sounding board, offering tremendous memories of wonderful times together on the ball fields of south-side Virginia.

I extend a special thank-you to Les Hall, who provided so many pictures of previous reunions along with his special brand of humor. I also want to acknowledge those who played years before my joining the team and those who followed me. My deepest appreciation goes out to the guys with whom I played those three glorious years. Their joy of the game of baseball and their acceptance of me as a member of the team make it one of the most cherished episodes of my life.

It would be calamitous to forget thanking the wives, girlfriends, and fans of the All-Stars. Their continued support and love for the Farmville All-Stars helped make the games so special. Their participation ensured the success of the team and helped nurture its legend.

Prologue

FOR A YOUNG BOY GROWING up in Alexandria, Virginia, the 1950s was a collection of enchanting opportunities. Alexandria and Northern Virginia were richly endowed with both neighborhood and nationally recognized sports venues, exceptional cultural options, and, of course, the good jobs of government. As early as I can remember, I wanted to play baseball, probably more than anything. More than that, I dreamed about the possibility of becoming a Major League pitcher. In my young life, everything else was certainly secondary. But my story, like the stories of us all, unfolded in a way I did not expect. How we all achieve our dreams, through circuitous paths and roadblocks, is the story of this book.

In the mid-1970s, I was a college professor in the Virginia town of Farmville in Prince Edward County. I was to become the first white baseball player to join the all–African American baseball team and, perhaps, the first white ballplayer in that Virginia league. While the story is about me, it is an even more poignant portrayal of my fellow teammates. In the years before I joined the Farmville All-Stars, my teammates had endured the civil strife that had engulfed our country and, in particular, their town. Rather than integrate, the Prince Edward County Board of Supervisors, in fierce opposition to the US Supreme Court's decision in *Brown v. Board of Education*, closed its schools for a long five years. The stories of how my teammates coped, rose above, and eventually accepted a white player on their team is what this book is about. It is also what America is about.

As teammates we found a way to fit an unusual puzzle together, although we might have been challenged by differences in skin color, educational and cultural opportunities, and baseball experiences. How we treated each other and how we were treated by other league players, the fans, and the general community are detailed in the narratives of the team, found at the end of the book. The narratives contain the memories of the former All-Stars, their wives, girlfriends, the fans, and community leaders. Their personal stories are often funny and sometimes chilling but always heartfelt. More often than not, all we wanted to do was enjoy the game of baseball on those sweltering summer weekends in south-side Virginia.

CHAPTER 1

Dick's Story

MY LOVE FOR THE GAME of baseball began in Alexandria, Virginia, a suburban community just across the Potomac River from Washington, DC, our nation's capital. As a young child, I grew up watching and reading about the Washington Senators, a professional American League team. During baseball season, I'd get up early to read the morning *Washington Post* to see how the Senators, a low-performing team, had fared the previous day. I rejoiced in their victory and suffered mightily in their losses, which were many. To this day, I still rise early to read about the Tampa Bay Rays, as I now live in Sarasota, Florida, which is a scant fifty miles from St. Petersburg, where the Rays play at the Trop, a.k.a. Tropicana Stadium. The Rays had a better team than the Senators, yet in 2015, they finished two games out of the cellar, last place!

Stimulated by my early involvement with the Senators, I wanted to try out for a Little League team at Simpson Field in Alexandria. At that time, the Little League was sponsored by the Alexandria Parks & Recreation Department. During the early fifties, the Parks and Rec also ran a summer recreation program at Beverly Park, known as the Gravel Pit or, more commonly, the Pit.

Our home was half a block away from heaven, the Pit. Why it was called "the Pit" is a mystery, as there's never been gravel there—just dirt, rocks, and tufts of grass. The Pit is a four- to five-acre plot of land in the sleepy community of Beverly Hills. All of the kids in the area would meet there daily to play baseball, football, or basketball, depending on the season. Soccer was not even on the horizon in the 1950s and 1960s. The Pit was carved out of the hillside when the small brick homes in the community were first being built in 1940. It's gratifying to know my sister still owns the house in which we grew up. She is one of the few original families who still own those charming little homes today. Who knows why the Pit was left without homes? The shape resembled a baseball stadium with a high hill forming the boundaries of the outfield. A crude field was fashioned out of the land as kids and adults came to play ball. Adults brought children and dogs there to walk and to use the swings and slide. Kids would use adjacent woods to play secret war games, hide-and-seek, and other games that kids have loved playing for years. During the summers, we'd have breakfast at home and meet at the Pit to involve ourselves in mayhem and joy, realizing we didn't have to be home until dinner. The Pit helped to hone pitching and batting skills, throwing and catching footballs, basketball layups, and free throws for thousands of kids over the years. At Christmas, the large cedar tree at one corner of the property was decorated with multicolored lights as carolers and neighbors sang Christmas tunes. It was an idyllic place to play and sharpen one's growing athletic skills. It was at the Pit that I hoped to develop my skills sufficiently to play Little League baseball. Thankfully, the Pit is still there today providing joy for multitudes of children and adults, although now it is adorned with a large asphalt area to accommodate trikes and bicycles. Gone is the treasured ball field, and trees now disrupt the football portion of the upper playground. Also missing is the basketball backboard. So contact sports have given way to more individual activities for young children.

My first foray into organized baseball was a disaster! For whatever reason, I failed the tryout for a Little League team at Simpson Field. If a reason was given for my dismissal, it's been long forgotten. The long walk home that afternoon was one of the worst things I had ever experienced, then or now. I was sure everyone was laughing at me. Yet that exclusion from Little League helped form a resolve in me to never fail again. My parents were supportive. Mom said she'd help me find another league. Dad, who divorced my mom when I was four, said he would continue to play catch with me when he would see my sister, BA, and me on weekends. Still, the pain existed until another league was found in Arlington, Virginia, an adjacent county. The practice

The Gravel Pit

and game field, Utah Field, was less than a mile from Shirlington—a small shopping community that is now a bustling array of restaurants and trendy shops. Utah Field is still in existence and boasts fencing, dugouts, manicured grass, and a rock less infield. I played for Glebe Road Baptist Church that summer, riding my bike to practice and games. As a pitcher, I won a few games, including a no-hitter of five to seven innings. I felt redeemed.

During those early years, I came up with an idea to help my pitching skills develop. I took a dark crayon and drew a large square on the outside brick wall of our garage. For years, I honed my pitching skills by throwing a tennis ball at the target. I imagined each pitch was crucial and practiced throwing to professional big-league players in All-Star, World Series, and regular-season games. This activity also helped my fielding skills. That simple activity of throwing at the target, I believe, helped me tremendously with my ball control in later years.

In seventh and eighth grade, I played for St. Rita's Elementary School baseball team as a pitcher. The team was coached by Mr. Brownlow, who had two children enrolled at the school. In one game, I had a no-hitter going into the final inning. Two outs later, the bases were loaded due to a walk and two

Garage wall at home

fielding errors. I worked the next batter count to three balls and two strikes. I made the sign of the cross, requesting help from God. All I needed to do to record the no-hitter was to get the next batter out. To my surprise and bewilderment, the batter at the plate made the sign of the cross too and, I assume, asked for divine intervention! What a conundrum! Whom was God going to listen to on this fateful afternoon? The next pitch was a strike, and I was showered with adulation from my teammates. I have reflected often on that moment as I've tried to understand how this wonderful universe operates and what my place is in the grand scheme of life. My dear friend Max and I have had long philosophical discussions on this topic, trying to make sense of the master plan, if there is one.

I returned to the dreaded Simpson Field for Junior Major League play in the late 1950s. My coach, Norman Grimm, was an excellent student of the game and taught our team many countless strategies. He spent many years as a detective with the Alexandria City Police Department, becoming an icon in the area. One year Coach Grimm sent me a birthday card! I was floored that he would single me out. I'm sure Coach Grimm did this for each player, making them feel special. I learned from him how important it is to be recognized and how easy it is to do so in a positive way. The team loved this man, with his firm approach to the game and his simple, positive recognition.

In 1966, I had the opportunity to coach in the Junior Major League at Simpson Field. Head Coach Hilton Davis and I had the chance to meet with Coach Grimm again as competitors. In the last inning, one of our batters hit a long ball to right field, driving in what was presumed to be the winning run. Our players erupted with joy at defeating a quality team in the league championship, if I am remembering correctly. After the game, Coach Grimm and I congratulated each other for a "game well played." Coach Grimm said, "You know, your runner missed third base as he was coming home." I asked why he didn't protest the oversight. He commented that our team was so overjoyed for winning that he didn't want to spoil our celebrations. He indicated it was only a game, and some things were more important than winning. Coach Grimm continued to have an impact on young and old ballplayers. I marvel at coaches like Norman Grimm who share countless hours with young men, helping them mature and find success in a wide variety of endeavors.

In my junior year at Francis C. Hammond High School, I played on the junior varsity team. While it wasn't varsity, I was able to pitch in many games. In one of those games, against the junior varsity team from Yorktown High School, I struck out fourteen batters in a seven-inning game that cemented a win for our team. I still have the baseball signed by Coach Herb Holt congratulating me for my efforts. That afternoon the varsity team returned from a losing effort against an opponent. A senior player, upon hearing of my exploits earlier that day, came to me and said he certainly wished I had been pitching for them! Again, the power of praise was so exhilarating. I do believe I could have struck out Mickey Mantle that day. Coach Holt and I would, years later, join forces as building-level administrators in the Alexandria City School Division.

Simpson Field in Alexandria

That summer, I tried out for and was accepted on the Post 24 American Legion team in Alexandria. The team combined some of the best players from Alexandria's two white high schools, George Washington and Francis C. Hammond. My role was to be a pitcher. I didn't have much speed, but I was blessed with a great curve ball and good control, helped immeasurably by those countless tennis balls thrown at our garage wall.

In my first game as a reliever, I was called in to the game in the last inning. We were up by one run with the count on the batter of three balls and two strikes. The bases were loaded. Bob Grove, the catcher, called for a fastball, which flew from my hand to his glove for a called third strike and a win for our team. I won six more games that summer in relief. I have to admit that I hoped our starting pitchers would make mistakes, give up runs, and put players on base, thus necessitating a relief pitcher. I just loved to pitch and wanted to play as much as I could. I truly believed I could get opposing batters out, especially with my teammates backing me up. They were tremendously gifted players, several of whom went on to play college ball.

We won the Northern Virginia District Championship and headed to Staunton, Virginia, to face the Shenandoah Valley district champions. We were anticipating an easy time dispensing of the "farm boys" in quick fashion, confident in our abilities. Several of the team members were walking around the city of Staunton prior to the game. We entered a local store where a male clerk talked to us and said, "I understand you have quite a relief pitcher." I was dumbstruck, and I'm sure I grew ten inches that day, realizing I had been singled out for scrutiny and praise. I was brimming with confidence and so looking forward to the game. Needless to say, they crushed us 28–5, and I was saddled with my first and only loss of the season. Their catcher, who was later drafted and played with the Pittsburgh Pirates, hit a line drive home run off me that, I believe, is still rising fifty-six years later. It was a long drive back to Alexandria after two crushing losses in Staunton.

Thankfully, we did end the season with another win against a strong Arlington Legion team. In that game, I was brought in as a reliever only to be ineffective. Coach Ray Struder walked calmly from the mound and told me to play second base while he brought in another pitcher. I had never played second base in my life and was scared to death, appealing to God not to have a ground ball come my way. An inning later, Coach Struder put me back in to pitch, and we won the game.

1960 Post 24 district champions. Author is in first row, third from right.

Coach Struder was a marvelous coach and a tremendous human being. He highlighted each player in the press releases he put out in the *Alexandria Gazette* after each game. He realized, too, how important positive reinforcement can be. Three years ago, I attempted to locate Coach Struder. I discovered that he had ended his career coaching the baseball and golf teams at Eastern Kentucky University. In my discussions with his wife, I learned that Ray had continued to be loved and cherished by the young men he coached. Former Eastern Kentucky players consistently sought him out for advice and good cheer after his career had ended. I am sorry I was too late to share stories and friendship with him. He left an indelible impact on me and so many others.

Having taken a course entitled Behavior Modification for my doctoral degree, I have a better understanding of the importance of positive reinforcement. Most of us are thrilled to receive it in all of its various forms, from verbal reinforcement to tangible reinforcers such as letter sweaters, jackets, trophies, and medals. At the end of our Legion play that summer of 1960, each player was awarded a distinctive black-and-yellow wool championship jacket from Post 24. These jackets were worn with a healthy dose of pride. My jacket, which still fits, hangs in a closet where it serves as a visual reminder of what a wonderful group of young men I had the opportunity to enjoy the wonderful game of baseball with! Not far from the jacket is a trophy for best pitcher I received from the Farmville All-Stars in 1976, a team that will be featured later in the book.

In 1961, Sid Hudson was the pitching coach for the Washington Senators. He had played for only two Major League teams, the Senators and the Boston Red Sox. Hudson had a lackluster career. He pitched his best in 1940, winning seventeen games and throwing two one-hitters. He was the runner-up for the Rookie of the Year award in 1940. Hudson was voted an all-star in 1941 and 1942.

During Hudson's tenure in Washington, my father contacted him to see if he would work with me on my desire to become a better pitcher. I remember driving to Griffith Stadium, then home of the Washington Senators in Northeast DC. As I got out of my car, I could smell the tremendous aroma of bread being baked up the street at the Wonder Bread factory. If I close my eyes today, I can still smell that fabulous scent. I was fascinated by the prospect of working with a true professional. I even contemplated the possibility that Hudson would see what a good pitcher I was and think of me "down the road" for a tryout with the Senators after completing high school.

Coach Hudson met me at the players' entrance and escorted me to the locker room. He told me to put on Marty Keough's uniform number twenty-five, which he used during his one year with the Senators. My mind was traveling a thousand miles an hour. There I was, putting on a Major League uniform and walking out on the field of Griffith Stadium. I had attended numerous baseball and football games over my formative years and had never been on the field itself. I almost felt like a Major Leaguer!

I wanted to look around at the spectacle of the stadium as seen from the grass of a Major League team, but I still needed to pay attention to what Coach Hudson was saying to me. After my heart stopped fluttering, I realized that Hudson had asked me to go through my throwing motion from the beginning to the end with no catcher present. I went through the motions I had used since I was a ten-year-old on the fields of Alexandria and Arlington, the garage wall, and the Pit. I kept waiting for the catcher to come out of the dugout so I could demonstrate my abilities to Coach Hudson. He then surprised me by telling me to go home, find a large mirror in my house, and practice my throwing technique with the changes he recommended in front of it! I was to do this exercise daily for as long as I could. My recollection is that he felt I had to have the proper routine etched deeply in my mind. It was, definitely, developing muscle memory. That was my first and last opportunity to step out on a Major League field; however, my mother's dressing mirror served me well for many afternoons of technique improvement!

I was still elated to have had the opportunity to visit a professional locker room and field at Griffith Stadium, put on a Major Leaguer's uniform, and receive advice from a Major League pitching coach. I'm sure I floated all the way home. There's no doubt in my mind that Coach Hudson's advice helped my form and effectiveness. He would not accept any money for the time he spent with me. I later discovered that my dad had sent Coach Hudson a twenty-five-dollar US savings bond. My guess is that Sid Hudson just wanted to give back to the baseball community that had been so supportive of his earlier foray into professional baseball. I will always treasure that afternoon with its numerous highlights for a young man who loved throwing a baseball above everything else. A special thank you goes out to Coach Hudson for his graciousness in helping one young man achieve his dream.

It was a heady time going into my senior year of baseball and another summer of Legion ball. I had hopes of earning a baseball scholarship to Duke University in Durham, North Carolina. Duke had a wonderful baseball program in the early 1960s. At that time, Alexandria's two white high schools had both fraternities and sororities. As fate would have it, I was kicked off the team before the beginning of the season. Athletes were told in the fall that if you were a member of a fraternity, you wouldn't be able to play sports. I was president of one of the fraternities and refused to quit. As the baseball season began, I was called into the coach's office, where I was told I was kicked off the team due to the fraternity issue. There went any chance for a Duke scholarship.

That spring, knowing that my final summer with Post 24 was upcoming, I did throw to Rusty Gardner, who would be the catcher for Post 24 during the summer, in order to be prepared for the season. In a strange twist of fate, the high-school baseball coach, Jerry Morris, asked me at the end of the team's season if I wanted to throw batting practice for the team. I readily accepted, hoping for some form of retribution and success. I had been "Peck's Bad Boy" in high school and wanted to go out with my head held high. I threw as if each pitch was 3–2 in the last inning. The batters couldn't get the ball out of the infield. Even the coach couldn't connect. Perhaps time has clouded my memories, and I don't believe he hit the ball out of the infield. I just felt somewhat vindicated and wished the fraternity issue hadn't ruined my possible career in baseball. The Post 24 summer season ended with a lackluster 4–2 pitching record for me.

It needs to be noted that throughout all my years playing organized or sandlot baseball, I had never faced an African American player or had one on my team. And the year was 1962, an important era for the civil rights movement that would have a significant effect on my life in rural Farmville, Virginia, several years later.

CHAPTER 2

College and Teaching

I WAS ACCEPTED TO THE University of Virginia in the fall of 1962 with hopes of making the baseball team in the spring of 1963. My meeting with Jim West, coach of the Cavaliers, was punctuated by his comments to do well academically the first semester.

Life at the university was a challenge for me. The opportunity to "raise hell" and take seventy-one road trips in the first seven months to see girls, coupled with my lack of willpower to study and attend classes, combined to make my stay in Charlottesville less than positive. Between road trips, partying at the fraternity houses, and a general malaise, my grades were horrific. I decided to leave the university at spring recess. In order to do so, I had to have an exit interview with Dean Runk, an imposing presence at the university. I found him to be a charming man who quietly asked me what I wanted to do with my life. When I mentioned a love of horses, he recommended that I spend whatever time was necessary to determine what was going to make my life come together.

I left the university in April of 1963 with an official letter stating that I was a member in good standing at the university, had a C in physical education, and would be welcome to return to Charlottesville in the future. Little did I know that just sixty miles south of Charlottesville, the board of supervisors of Prince Edward County had closed their entire public school system rather than integrate. That decision would affect over 1,500 students for five years and would have a serious impact on my baseball career and my outlook on life.

Armed with the letter from the University of Virginia and three credits in physical education, I was admitted to American University in Washington, DC, on a probationary status in the summer of 1963. I settled into my studies at AU and looked forward to playing baseball and joining a fraternity, Alpha Tau Omega. At that time, freshmen were not allowed to play varsity sports, and there were no freshman or junior varsity baseball teams. I developed bursitis in my right arm from throwing to my dad, which eliminated playing my sophomore year. In my junior year at AU, I experienced a losing season, going 0–3. We had a fair team that just never jelled. I did, however, earn a varsity letter jacket for my exploits. I was able, years later in Farmville, Virginia, to resurrect that jacket and my baseball career in a most unlikely way.

My senior season never materialized. After being married in 1966, I was eagerly anticipating my final year of college baseball. I still entertained the idea of a career in baseball and knew this was my last opportunity. And then, my life changed. I received a letter from the US Selective Service informing me that I was to be inducted into the armed services on December 21, 1966. Gary, one of my fraternity brothers, told me he had received a deferment due to the fact that he was teaching in a local school system. I investigated this situation, and my wife and I both applied for teaching positions even though neither of us had had any teaching experience or education classes. We were interviewed by the personnel director of a Northern Virginia school district. A few days later, I received a call from the personnel director stating that he was offering my wife a teaching position but couldn't hire me. I thanked him for the call and told him my wife couldn't accept the position unless I was also hired. The director relented and offered us both positions. Mine involved teaching fifth grade, while my wife accepted a position teaching art at the high school.

I only took this course of action as I knew I wouldn't be able to graduate until the end of summer school in August 1967. Without the teaching deferment, I would have been inducted when my class graduated in June.

I started teaching fifth grade with no teaching experience or classes in education. I observed the departing teacher for two days and was thrust into the position. I taught from 8:00 a.m. to 4:00 p.m. and took twelve hours of business undergraduate classes in night school at American University Mondays through Thursdays. There went my chance to play baseball, the sport that I so dearly loved, in my senior year.

In order to receive my BS in business, I had to complete eighteen hours in summer school that year. The dean of the business school doubted I could do all of this academically or physically based on my previously unremarkable academic career. He wagered a bet that I would not be able to graduate in August, and I accepted his challenge with relish. As it turned out, I made the best grades of my college life and graduated that August. I had already signed a contract to continue teaching for the upcoming school year; however, I was ready to be drafted after graduation. The Vietnam War was demanding more and more troops, so I contacted my local draft board, explaining to them I had now acquired my degree and was eligible to be drafted into the service. To my surprise, I continued receiving deferments, and my love of teaching continued to grow.

My dad was a remarkable man who knew the value of an education. He had received a bachelor's degree from Toledo University and a master's degree from American University. He challenged me to continue with my studies. He said that, rather than going bowling one night a week, I take graduate courses in education since I liked teaching so much. He offered to pay for any graduate course I took and passed, plus he'd pay ten dollars for books! Each course completed would merit a seventy-five-dollar check. At that time, in the late 1960s and early 1970s, graduate education classes at the University of Virginia were sixty-six dollars for a three-credit course, and books rarely exceeded ten dollars.

So it was off to teaching during the day and one night class a week. Often the courses were only offered on the grounds at the university in Charlottesville. My schedule now included a two-hour drive from Northern Virginia to Charlottesville after school ended, a three-hour night class, and a two-hour drive back to Northern Virginia. After two years of this hectic schedule, I received a MEd in elementary school administration. Thoughts of playing baseball again dwindled. My only attempt at the sport came in a reunion game at American University in the late sixties, and that was only a one-inning stint of pitching to allow more people to participate. I figured these reunion games would be my only opportunity to play the game I so dearly loved. Just when you think you've got life figured out, things change!

I taught fifth grade for two and a half years at Rippon Elementary School in Woodbridge, Virginia, and enjoyed the curriculum and the children at that age. I must mention a poignant yet serious situation I found myself in as I first started teaching. Having no education background, I was, basically, at the mercy of the teacher's edition of each of the reading and text books. There, in red print in the teacher's manual, were teacher suggestions for what to say to the children. Without those prompts, I would have been lost. The children thought I was brilliant; I thought I was lucky as hell.

Since I desired to eventually become an elementary principal, I thought it would be wise to teach a younger grade. What a mistake I made. The third-grade class to which I was assigned was a nightmare. The children's needs were greater than my ability to handle their pressing problems. After a few weeks, I requested a transfer to another grade. My wish was granted, and so I transferred to a fourth-grade class at nearby Featherstone Elementary School. The kids were great, and I adapted quickly to the age of the students. The fourth-grade class was adorable, and so I requested to teach the same class the following year in fifth grade. I believe all of the parents opted to have me teach their children in fifth grade.

At the end of that year, I decided to move to Fairfax County, an adjoining county with a better-paying system in a much larger district. I applied for a third-grade position at Hybla Valley Elementary School. My previous experience in fourth and fifth grade helped tremendously in teaching third grade. This time I was prepared. I had five reading groups going throughout the year, with bright and challenging children. It was a marvelous teaching and learning experience for me. Anthony and Tyrone were two children who were especially difficult and enjoyable at the same time. I often wonder where these children, now adults, are and how they have fared!

During the late spring semester of 1970, the University of Virginia initiated a doctoral program in early-childhood education. This was a new endeavor for the university, and few men were interested in the program both at Virginia and nationally. I'd had the opportunity of teaching third, fourth, and fifth grades during the previous five years and liked the elementary and early-childhood levels. I applied for and was accepted into the doctoral program in 1971, the year my son was born. I moved our family to Charlottesville that summer to commence my graduate work in early-childhood education. Being a graduate assistant allowed me to teach courses for the School of Education for undergraduate and graduate students. I also spent a half year as an assistant to Mrs. Berta Wood in her preschool in Charlottesville. Berta was an outstanding teacher/director of her program for preschool children. Her technique and European early-childhood materials were outstanding, and I gained valuable experience while at Beau Pre School.

While walking to class one day on the grounds (campus) at the university, I ran into an old nemesis, Dan Murdaugh. Dan had been my assistant principal at Hammond High School years earlier. We chatted and walked. Our conversation shifted to education and why I was at the university. It turned out that Dan was the director of continuing education at the university and was looking for someone to teach graduate-level extension classes throughout the commonwealth. My first foray into extension class instruction began in Dinwiddie County in south-side Virginia. For the next seven years, I served as an adjunct professor for the university teaching graduate education classes from the Eastern Shore of Virginia to Roanoke and points in between. Dan and I became fast friends and I was asked to be his Trustee upon his demise. He was a friend and a mentor and is sorely missed.

After two years of course work at the university, teaching as an adjunct professor, and service as the director of Sabot School, an early learning center situated between Richmond and Charlottesville, I accepted an offer to teach early-childhood and education courses as an assistant professor at Longwood College in Farmville, Virginia, in 1973. I vividly remember being offered $10,000 for the position. Summoning all of my negotiating skills, I held out for $10,500! In 1974, while teaching at Longwood College, I received my doctor of education degree (Ed.D) from the University of Virginia. Little did I know that some of the worst and some of the best times of my life lay directly ahead!

CHAPTER 3
Civil Rights

As EARLY AS 1896, US Supreme Court decisions would begin having effects on civil rights issues in the United States. The *Plessy v. Ferguson* decision that year established the concept of "separate but equal," allowing school divisions to segregate the races if the school facilities, materials, supplies, and teachers were equal in quality. The problem was they weren't!

For years, African Americans suffered mightily under these conditions. In 1951, students at Moton High School in Farmville, Virginia, began questioning the physical condition of their school, the materials available to them, the quality of the buses bringing children to school, and the teaching staff credentials. Students at Moton High School, under the leadership of Barbara Johns, a senior, initiated a peaceful protest by leading the high-school students to walk out, protesting the lack of adequate school facilities, the quality of educational materials available, and the caliber and size of the teaching staff. Through this peaceful demonstration, the students of Moton hoped to highlight their plight on a state and national level, determined to end years of African American students being overlooked. These activities did bring attention to this rural community located in Prince Edward County in central Virginia. The actions initiated by these high-school students did attract both statewide and national attention—so much so that Prince Edward County was enjoined in a suit brought to the US Supreme Court in 1954.

The famous case *Brown v. Board of Education* brought together several entities who were trying to end the separate but equal doctrine found in *Plessy v. Ferguson*. The Supreme Court ruled that segregation was unconstitutional and ordered all public schools to open their doors to African American students. School divisions across the country were slow to accept this decision. In 1959, several school divisions in Virginia refused to integrate, including the cities of Charlottesville and Norfolk and Warren and Prince Edward counties. After being closed for a year, Charlottesville, Norfolk, and Warren school divisions reopened their schools to all students. Only Prince Edward County remained closed, refusing to fund the public school system. The Supreme Court continued to press the issue, finally ordering Prince Edward County to integrate their schools in 1959. That same year, the two white high schools in Alexandria, Virginia, admitted African American students. Two black students were admitted in February 1959 to both George Washington and Francis C. Hammond High Schools. The board of supervisors of Prince Edward County again refused to fund the public school system, forcing the schools to remain closed.

At the same time, Prince Edward Academy in Farmville was opened, accepting only white students. Funds allocated for the public school system via state and federal funding were used to help defray some of the costs to the academy through tax credits. Massive resistance to integration was championed by then-governor J. Lindsay Almond and US Senator Robert Byrd. Schools were shuttered for five long years for African American students, from 1959 to 1964. For those five years, children and families struggled with the decision to close the schools. Some children were sent out of the county to live with other family members in order to attend school; some children were educated in local church settings; some were schooled in individual homes, and some did not attend school at all for five years! For those students who left the area to live with other family members or friends of the family, the effects would linger for years, if not forever. The fabric of their lives would be damaged in numerous ways for countless years.

Over fifteen hundred children and families were adversely affected by the decision to keep the schools segregated and closed. These children are referred to as the "lost generation." There was no access to formal education if they remained in Farmville/Prince Edward County. No other public school system in the United States kept its schools closed rather than integrate. Quite a sad commentary for this quaint little community in rural Virginia.

Finally, in 1963, some of the schools, known as free schools, opened on a temporary basis to help children transition back into a public school environment. Volunteers came from across the United States to Prince Edward County to help serve as teachers. Supplies were minimal, and classrooms were in need of maintenance and renovation after years of being closed and neglected. Though some of the schools were opened, it was chaotic for students, teachers, and parents. Records were missing; the original teachers had left the area to search for other teaching positions, and children were misplaced in grade levels that were inappropriate for their age and ability. Many students just didn't attend any schooling for five years and eventually entered school not knowing how to read, write, and use basic arithmetic.

Ricky Brown, a coauthor of this book, tells the story of getting on an elevator at the local department store in Farmville not knowing how to operate it. As a five-year-old, he only knew how to spell his name. He started pressing buttons until the elevator started moving. Eventually, he hit the red button that stopped the elevator between floors. At some point, he pressed the correct button and was able to exit the elevator. A frightening experience for a young child.

Other children and students can offer stories of not being prepared to graduate from high school when they returned to school. Lorenzo Clark, a truly gifted athlete, tells of not being able to play baseball in his senior year due to Virginia state age requirements. He was still drafted by the Baltimore Orioles and played in their farm system, eventually being traded to the Washington Senators. An injury blocked his efforts to make it to the Major Leagues. Many of the narratives of individuals affected by such a long closure of the schools are included in this book, helping to showcase the dramatic consequences of the county's actions.

During this five-year period, most of the rest of the country was unaware of the plight of African American children being denied their right to public education. Even though I attended the University of Virginia in Charlottesville, a mere sixty miles away, I did not know the tragedies the children and families were experiencing in this rural community. I suspect that most people in the United States, unless they were impacted by this callous decision, had never heard of Prince Edward County and the school closings. It was under the John F. Kennedy administration that these events started to be publicized. To this day, most Americans are still unaware that Prince Edward County closed their schools rather than integrate. This decision to not fund integrated schools would have deep and lasting consequences for all Americans of any race.

For some, the wounds are deep, while for others, they are just below the surface. Ricky Brown, a valued member of the community, felt that God chose Prince Edward County to carry the burden of the closings because they were strong in their faith and in the belief that they could overcome the tragedies being inflicted on them. There were no riots; no civil disobedience other than sit-ins at local restaurants or trying to attend white-only churches; no burning or trashing of property, just a quiet resolve to move ahead, living life to the fullest.

When the schools reopened in 1964, there was mass confusion. Children's previous school records had been lost or destroyed, and teachers had long moved from the area to find jobs outside of Prince Edward County. For all intents and purposes, the schools were well over 90 percent populated by African Americans. School facilities needed major renovations, buses needed complete maintenance, teaching materials, supplies, and equipment had to be procured, and teachers needed to be recruited. Prince Edward County school children were struggling to keep their heads above water academically.

While the schools were technically integrated, there was a great deal of resentment arising from the treatment African Americans had received prior to, during, and after the schools had closed. It was this mind-set that the Farmville All-Stars and I would face as we collided on a baseball field in the mid-1970s. Looking back on these developments, it is apparent to me that they showed their grace, dignity, and strength in dealing with a white college professor who wanted to join their team.

What has struck me in writing this book and in the interviews I've conducted is the resilience of the African American community in dealing with the closing of the schools and the disruption of children having to move to other towns or cities outside of Virginia to live with relatives in order to attend school. As I mentioned earlier, more than one All-Star told me that God picked Prince Edward County to endure these hardships because he knew they could! Their individual and collective personas helped them cope with the blatant disregard for the US Supreme Court's 1954 ruling that public schools had to be integrated across the country. When I tried to press the issue, players said they felt that their faith and belief in God helped them put aside feelings of anger and despair.

During the course of my interview with Reverend Samuel Williams, a civil rights leader in Farmville, I felt that emotions and feelings were still sensitive issues within the African American community. He left me with the feelings that all was not well in the town and county believing that much needed to be done to assuage the hurt, rancor, and disregard for justice that was perpetuated by many in the white community.

Gerald Spates, the town manager for over thirty-five years, said that he felt race relations had improved greatly over the years. He noted that when he took over his position in 1973 he focused on the infrastructure in the black community. Sewers, water lines, and roads all needed attention, repair, and maintenance. Gerald felt that relations with Longwood University have continued to improve; however, the university is growing and expanding into the African American community.

I think the overriding factor for the All-Stars is to let the past stay in the past. The inequities of the 1950s through the 1970s are, for the most part, gone. Black and white citizens have improved relationships and strive to work together on issues continuing to confront them.

CHAPTER 4

The Farmville All-Stars

SO, WHO ARE THE FARMVILLE All-Stars? By most accounts, the team was formed in 1960 under the leadership of John Bracey, the first coach/manager. Players from different teams joined to form the All-Stars. From its inception, the All-Stars team was an amalgam of players and personalities ranging in age from late teens to midforties. Gilbert Scott, one of the original All-Stars, had previously played for a team in Prospect, Virginia. Gilbert, now in his eighties, was tremendously helpful in describing the team's initial year. The All-Stars were a collection of men and teenagers who excelled at playing the "national pastime," baseball. They were businessmen, high-school and college players, carpentry and construction workers, store employees, officers who worked for the sheriff's department and the department of corrections, and some who were unemployed. The one thing they had in common was their love for the game.

In central and south-central Virginia, opportunities for African Americans to engage in social activities were limited. The All-Stars provided an avenue for them to engage in sports and display their God-given talents. The players and the African American community looked forward to the weekends in the summer so they could attend games and cheer and/or play the game of baseball. It was "The Thing" to do on weekends. On Saturday and Sunday afternoons, baseball fields across south-side Virginia became a social haven for fans and players who loved the game, the atmosphere, and the opportunity to be seen. It was their time to root for their team during a time of unsettled integration issues.

Players and fans would travel many miles to face other teams in adjoining towns and communities. On occasion, the All-Stars would travel far afield, including trips to Falls Church, Virginia, a suburb of Washington, DC; Richmond, Virginia; and even a trip to Newark, New Jersey.

It was not uncommon for the All-Stars to play thirty-five to forty games a year, and they went undefeated in many of those years. Several of the All-Stars commented that they had a presence that caused many of their opponents to seem defeated even before the game began. Most games played to an audience of one hundred to three hundred fans, and it was quite a spectacle to see car after car pull into home and away games, with players and fans ready to do battle with opposing teams.

Through their first fifteen years, the Farmville All-Stars were an all-black team playing in an all-black league. The games provided a relief from the turmoil certainly going on in the Farmville/Prince Edward community. The school-closing episode had recently taken place, and the entire African American community was attempting to deal with the consequences. Baseball provided a relief for this segment of the population in the Farmville area. There was no bloodshed during the peaceful protests, yet there was animosity seething just under the surface. After all, everyone in the community was affected in some manner—black and white. While there had been little to no violence, feelings in the black community had been trampled by segments of the white population.

It was with great humility and thankfulness that I ventured onto the home field of the All-Stars one spring day in the mid-1970s. While I was no longer naive to the problems encountered by African Americans and the school closings, I approached the All-Stars with hope and great anticipation. After fifteen years of playing as an all-African American team, the All-Stars were about to encounter a white professor from Longwood College who had an intense desire to play baseball. Later in the book, you will meet Lorenzo, Ricky, Les, Walter, Hilton, Bug, Sheep Dog, and others. These players, like the ones who preceded them and followed them, had one thing in common: they loved to play baseball, and they were excellent at it!

The team eventually ceased playing in 1986, with many of the guys going on to play softball. Periodically, reunions have been held where All-Stars from earlier teams and those who played until the final out was recorded shared an afternoon reliving past glories and few defeats. It has been my distinct pleasure to have attended a few of these wonderful occasions where stories are shared with laughter, grace, and hearty embellishments. There is just something about baseball and guys that brings generations together.

In my wildest dreams, I never would have thought that I would become a Farmville All-Star, the first white player in the team's history!

CHAPTER 5

Acceptance

AFTER I RESTORED MY NINETEENTH-CENTURY farmhouse and taught at Longwood College for a few years, my mind wandered, looking for something in which to become active. Although I had not played baseball for almost ten years, I managed to stay in shape with long-distance running and tennis.

I started slowly with the running by trying to make it to the front gate on our property, a whopping quarter mile. Once that distance was conquered, I gradually extended the runs to four or five miles. Eventually, I entered my first marathon race in Richmond, Virginia, planning to quit at the five-mile marker. I felt too good to stop there and decided to see how far I could run. I knew as I approached the fifteen-mile marker that I wouldn't have enough strength or willpower to continue. I set my sights on an elderly gentleman ahead of me and sprinted as best I could to beat him to that mile marker. As I slowly passed this aged man, he said, "Go get them, young man." I reached the fifteen-mile marker and bent over in exhaustion. Just as I did, the elderly gentleman I had just passed blew by me in his steady gait, and I yelled encouragement to him. Later in life, I would complete four Marine Corps Marathon runs that featured running through Washington, DC, and ending at the Iwo Jima Marine Corps statue in Northern Virginia.

I also played a little tennis, but my heart was still focused on baseball even though I hadn't played for close to ten years. In the mid-1970s, I started searching for an adult baseball league to join. I felt that joining a team would keep me active and would introduce me to new people in the community. To my surprise, I could find no baseball teams in the area. It seems that my white adult friends preferred playing softball, and that wouldn't do for me. I wanted to play baseball. Once again, baseball slipped through my fingers.

There were no public preschool centers in the Farmville area. Realizing that my son needed a caring, safe environment, I decided to search the community to determine if there was a need for competent child care. My efforts paid off when I met Vera Allen, a member of the Martha E. Forrester Association. This group had access to an old school building that was vacant and in need of assistance. The board of the association was open to forming a preschool operation in the building, and I received permission to begin searching for personnel to run the operation and children to fill the building. The Forrester Association was extremely helpful to me as the concept grew into a reality through their moral and financial help. I hired a director, wrote a grant proposal to the US government to cover salary and benefits for an aide, purchased materials for equipment and supplies, enlisted the voluntary assistance of students studying early-childhood education at nearby Longwood College, and secured sufficient children of all races for the early learning center.

Trust me, the Lord works in mysterious ways! As I was leaving the center one afternoon, I noticed that a baseball diamond across the street was active with guys engaged in batting and fielding practice. I looked closer and saw that not only were the players African Americans, they were playing baseball! I immediately walked across the street and asked who was in charge. I was directed to Ricky Brown and Lorenzo Clark. These two men were the player-leaders of the All-Stars. The coach, Boo Jackson, was not at this practice.

This was a true sandlot team of guys in the Farmville/Prince Edward County community. Little did I realize that this team had been playing baseball for many years and had amassed an incredible record. It was not uncommon for them to go for an entire season of thirty to thirty-five games without a loss. They were the Yankees of baseball in south-side Virginia. The All-Stars were an eclectic grouping of players with diverse backgrounds. Some were married with children, while others were footloose and fancy free. The common thread of this fabric was that they all loved baseball, as did I! And the whole community loved and respected the All-Stars.

I had little idea of the strife the community and the team had been through with the closing of the schools. Children lost five years of education, families were turned upside down, and the civil rights of African Americans had been trampled by some of the white community. In addition, Longwood College had taken over many parcels of land and buildings through eminent domain. It was in the shadow of these issues and attitudes that I naively walked up to talk with Lorenzo and Ricky to ask about trying out for the All-Stars. I mentioned my past experiences with the American Legion team and my year at American University, hoping to impress them and show that I might be of help to the team. With everything that had occurred over the previous fifteen years and beyond, it would have been easy for the team to reject my request for a tryout; they had every right to do so. But the contempt that could have been sent my way never presented itself. Instead, their reply was to come out for the next practice and they'd take a look at me.

I was elated, telling the guys I'd be there for their next practice to throw on the sideline or perhaps throw batting practice. I scurried home to search for my glove and cleats, finding them packed away, seemingly for eternity. I pulled them out of an old box, cleaned them up, and started thinking about what might come next. The afternoon for their next practice day came slowly as I nervously waited for my opportunity to throw a baseball again.

I met Ricky and Lorenzo at the same field and proceeded to warm up. It had been a number of years since I had last pitched, and I had no idea how my arm would hold up. I started out slowly, throwing gently to prepare my arm for the serious part of the tryout. As my speed started its slow progression upward, my curve ball returned as if it had just been sleeping, waiting for this day to begin. After a number of pitches, it was evident to me that all those days and nights of throwing at the target on the garage wall were paying off.

One thing you need to know about the All-Stars is that positions seemed to belong to individual players. Lorenzo was the shortstop, a position he'd play until he was too old, injured himself, or was abducted by aliens. There was no platooning. It was rare for someone to take another man's position. They were all so good at what they did that you just had to wait for a position to come open in order to play. Pitching was a bit different, though, as the All-Stars played so many games during the late spring and summer that another pitcher could easily be added.

Ricky, Lorenzo, and I talked a bit about pitching and then, as I remember, they said they'd be happy for me to join the team. I was elated. I'm not sure everyone else was. The reception from the rest of the team ranged from "that's cool" to silence. I really didn't know what to expect and hoped for a cordial welcome from the All-Stars, but for the most part, my welcome and acceptance were tepid. I was clueless. Having grown up in a white suburban community with no experience competing with or against African Americans, I didn't see the All-Stars as a black team within a black league. I was just happy to be playing baseball again with a good, professional group of guys. It was a dream come true, but little did I realize that it would take some time to prove my worth to the team.

I didn't know then that I was the first white man to play for the All-Stars (other white players would be added in subsequent years) and perhaps the first white player in the all-black league. While many members of the team were cool to me, that gradually changed as we continued to win ball games when I pitched. Of course, we also won ball games when I didn't pitch! Even a school administrator at the college was skeptical of my playing on an all-black team, stating that "it might not look right for me or the college." I dismissed his comments and continued playing. We continued winning, which goes a long way in overcoming prejudices.

Sam "Bug" Gilliam, a great outfielder, was one of the teammates who had been slow to accept me as a member of the team. My "whiteness" stood out on the field, especially as a pitcher. While we were playing a game at the local high school, the competing team was giving me a particularly difficult time, verbally harassing me. The racially motivated verbiage was disturbing. For the first time in my life, I experienced an ounce of the tons of discrimination showered on my teammates from local and nationwide negative elements of our society. I said nothing in response to the shouted comments of our opponents or their fans and focused on the next batter. Finally, when the crescendo of abuse continued, Bug jumped out of the dugout with a baseball bat in hand, walked to our opponents' bench, and shouted for all to hear, "Keep the cracks down. He's our pitcher and a member of the All-Stars. The next guy who gives him a hard time will have to go through me!" That was it. Not a word of anger or derision was shouted at me for the rest of the game.

Although my memory is not the best anymore, I do believe that was the last time I experienced any grief at a game. There were good-natured jabs from many over the years after that, and they were all humorous and well intentioned. I had found a home, complete with friends and eager opponents who always wanted to win against me. I had been accepted as an All-Star.

It struck me how perverse discrimination can be. I thought to myself, "Dislike me because I can strike you out, not because of the color of my skin." What a revelation, and what an injustice African Americans had to endure for so many generations. I have often thought of that day when things weren't going my way. One must persevere in spite of what comes your way. The alternative is not an option.

And the beat went on. It was an absolute joy playing with the All-Stars during my three-year stint with the team. Acceptance from the team gradually grew to friendship, and we continued to win ball games. And they loved to give me grief. I remember pulling up to the Cumberland field for an afternoon of practice. It was a delightful summer afternoon. The windows on my car were down, and I had an eight-track tape of Earth, Wind & Fire blaring out of the speakers. When I pulled up to park, several of the players were yelling such things as "Look at that white boy and his tunes." I shut them up by offering beer out of the backseat cooler! It was fun being with friends!

We won so many games because these players were larger than life. Each player was quite talented and knew it without being brash. Ricky Brown was a cocaptain of the team and a gifted athlete who played football, basketball, and baseball in high school. He was primarily a catcher and could play any position with authority. His gregarious nature kept us all in stitches. From the first time I met him, he's been one of the happiest people I've ever known. He's become a respected member of the Farmville/Prince Edward County community. Without much effort, he's become a mentor for hundreds of young people in and out of the school system. I am honored to coauthor this book with Ricky. His laugh and sense of humor have only grown through the years. It's an honor to call him my friend.

Walter Brown is Ricky's older brother. Walter was a great defensive player, especially in the outfield, but he could also always be counted on to pitch when necessary. He was a quiet warrior who spoke loudly with his bat and glove. Walter loved baseball and his teammates. He gave his best every time he stepped onto the field.

Lorenzo "Hot Dog" Clark, a cocaptain of the team, was the finest player with whom I've ever had the good fortune to share the game. He was the most fluid player on our team, and I never saw anyone who could match his power, speed, and sense of the game. Hot Dog, as he liked to be called, could hit the ball with power and cover the infield as the shortstop with grace and ease. He may have been the fastest pitcher on the team. Hot Dog loved his name and lived up to it in every game he played. When you needed a hit or a defensive gem, he would do it! It's no wonder he was drafted by the Baltimore Orioles and played in their system until being injured. He had the essence of what you'd expect in a Major Leaguer. And yet, he's a quiet man who loves being a part of his community.

Les Hall was, and is, larger than life. He's a big man who carries himself with bravado and a quietness that is disarming. A fabulous catcher and first baseman, Les, I believe, enjoyed hitting home runs more than any other aspect of the game. And he has the gift of gab. I felt sorry for batters when they stepped up to the plate. Les let them know that they were destined to fail against whomever was pitching. I can still hear his bantering against batters and his own teammates—the latter, good-naturedly. If I was in a jam, Les would walk out to the mound to talk with me. I expected words of advice to get the batter out. Instead, he'd tell me that he was looking forward to a beer after the inning was over. He knew just what to say. He always seemed like a big bear that could tear your head off instead of the remarkably peaceful man he was then and is now. My favorite memory is Les riding up on his motorcycle in his uniform ready for a beer and the game.

Samuel "Bug" Gilliam holds a special place in my memories of the glorious years with the team. His standing down an entire team and fan base in support of me sets him apart. That gesture meant so much to me and helped cement my relationship with the rest of the team. His defensive skills in the outfield were legendary. He just caught anything hit anywhere near him. He was quiet and reserved then and is today. He's now retired and thoroughly enjoys playing golf.

Edward "Carew" Thornton was a tremendous second baseman. He didn't play all of the three years I did, but played before and after me. I would like to have played more with him as he was a good athlete, good student, a gifted musician, a 4.5 tennis player, an accountant, and an all-around good guy. And what a sense of humor! During one of the group interviews held in the summer of 2015, tears rolled down our faces as Edward brought up story after story, from being offered a scholarship to a prestigious local college to watching a Ku Klux Klan cross burning. Edward had speed, which helped him on defense and offense. He treated me fairly, and I wish we could have had more summers of ball playing together.

Willie Blanton was a presence in the outfield. Like Edward Thornton, he didn't play the same years I did. I remember him as a husky young man with a forever smile. Willie played left field, and few balls eluded him. He told me a story this past summer of when someone hit a ball into the brush and small trees. He retrieved the ball and threw it in to Lorenzo, who threw the runner out at home. In reality, the batter had probably hit a home run, but without specific ground rules, everybody just played the ball the best they could…or the best they could get away with! Willie came to the 2015 reunion with his still-warm smile. He's retired now from serving in several high-level positions with the Commonwealth of Virginia. And he's a proud PaPa!

Carl "Sally" Robinson played the infield for the All-Stars. Although he is now deceased, I wanted to share with readers what a powerful player he was. Sally brought power to the game. Some of his home runs were legendary. He and Les loved the competition between them and others over who could hit the longest homer. A large man, Sally was the epitome of a gentle man. He was big and never tried to intimidate people. He just played the game he loved with power and dignity. I still remember his smile, which could light up the entire field. It was Sally's passing that made me initially think about writing a book about the All-Stars. It was a hard loss for all of his teammates and fans.

These are just a few of those marvelous men and teenagers with whom I had the privilege of playing baseball. They made me feel accepted and appreciated and do so to this day.

Over a three-year period, I won twenty-two straight games with the All-Stars. I did, though, lose my final game to a good team visiting from Maryland…a difficult way to end my tenure with the team. I left Longwood and Farmville in 1979, returning eventually to Northern Virginia where my life and baseball career had begun. I found an adult league and team in Arlington where I pitched and won three more games before "hanging up my cleats" for good!

As I mentioned, other white players were accepted on the All-Stars roster. My guess is that they, like me, found a great cadre of individual players with an abiding desire to win. Quite simply, the Farmville All-Stars were winners in baseball and in the game of life. When faced with racial discrimination all around them, they accepted me and other white players to share the game we all so loved. Who would figure that their sense of decency surpassed even their love of the game and their ability to win? I have such fond memories of my time with the All-Stars. They accepted a white guy from Longwood College and opened my eyes and heart to a group of young and older men who were proud of who they were and what they could do with a baseball, bat, and glove.

As the years passed, story after story was told and sometimes embellished. What a joy it is to remain an All-Star forty years later. Ricky, Les, Lorenzo, and I have stayed in touch over the years. On visits to Farmville, I would look them up or talk with them over the phone. E-mails, eventually, would help us stay in touch. Reunions were held, some players moved out of the area, some passed away. In fact, Robert Lewis Carter was interviewed for the book in the summer of 2015, and he sat with me at the September reunion that year, only to pass in November. What remains are good friendships developed so long ago and nurtured by curled and fading photographs and the realization that all of us were willing to break barriers. I was just a guy who played with a great group of men and boys who wanted to play baseball and win. They excelled at both. More importantly, they made a difference to all around them. Efforts are under way to form a Farmville All-Stars Foundation to fund scholarships for needy students of all ages in Farmville/Prince Edward County to help ensure that their legacy of support to the community lives on!

CHAPTER 6
Differences

WERE THERE DIFFERENCES BETWEEN THE All-Stars and me? A few, for certain. I grew up in Alexandria, Virginia, a quaint city featuring eighteenth- and nineteenth-century homes just across the Potomac River from Washington, DC. In the 1960s, the population was under one million in the District of Columbia (DC) and surrounding counties and cities. Farmville's population hovered around three thousand during the summer and swelled to about five thousand when Longwood College students were in attendance during the school year. Farmville was quite a sleepy town during the summer months when the college was closed or only offering limited classes. Farmville is probably best known for being located between the sites of the Civil War's last battle at Sailor's Creek and the surrender of General Robert E. Lee's Army of Northern Virginia to General Ulysses S. Grant at Appomattox, Virginia.

There was always a plethora of things to do in Alexandria and DC, with national theaters offering Broadway plays, musicals, and comedy. The Washington Redskins, a National Football League team, operated at Griffith Stadium in the fall and winter, while the Washington Senators utilized the stadium from April through September. Professional basketball and soccer would not grace the scene until the early 1970s. There was a wide range of colleges and universities serving the area, including Georgetown University, George Washington University, American University, the University of Maryland, and Howard University. Movie theaters seemed to be on every corner—Alexandria had five of them—and there was the iconic Alexandria Skating Rink. All skate!

The District of Columbia was also home to the Smithsonian Institution, a truly wonderful group of museums incorporating science, history, geography, and aircraft from the Wright brothers' plane to Skylab and a space capsule. On the National Mall were the National Gallery of Art, with its priceless art pieces from paintings and sculptures to furniture and textiles, and numerous monuments of grandeur, including the Lincoln Memorial and its reflecting pool, as well as the Washington Monument. The Vietnam and World War II memorials would be added later. Just off the Mall was the Jefferson Memorial. There were also numerous small and prestigious museums, as well as drama and theater venues and a small but representative zoo.

Washington is also home to our three branches of government: the executive branch located in the White House, the legislative branch operating in the two houses of Congress in the Senate and House of Representatives, and the judicial branch housed in the Supreme Court. Washington is one of the premier cities in the world and for years was considered the hub of the free world. Foreign countries, large and small, have embassies within the limits of the District of Columbia.

Farmville had one theater, one drive-in theater, and cultural events at both Longwood and Hampden-Sydney Colleges. There was Walker's Diner, an icon that still serves great food to this day, and a paved landing strip for small planes. In addition, Prince Edward County was home to Twin Lakes State Park. Oddly enough, whites used one lake while blacks used the other.

The year 1959 proved to be an important one for the civil rights movement in the United States. This was the year the Prince Edward County Board of Supervisors refused to fund the public schools rather than integrate them. Schools in Alexandria were finally integrated in that year when African Americans Patsy and James Ragland enrolled in Francis C. Hammond High School. A letter from the Hammond PTA president (included in this book) informed parents about the impending integration of the school and ensured that high standards of the school would be maintained. On the Raglands' first day of school, security was tight at Hammond; there was a police presence, and teachers had to show identification. No incidents occurred other than a fire drill. The word around school that day was that a bomb threat had been received. There is no official acknowledgement of this alleged event. George Washington High School (GW) and other elementary schools also enrolled African Americans that month. There were no disruptions for the rest of the year. Patsy and James

Ragland settled in to the routine of normal students at a normal high school. In fact, James was offered membership to Kappa Psi Kappa fraternity, a local Hammond fraternity, but he declined. Parker-Gray, the African American high school in Alexandria, remained segregated until 1965 when it was closed and all three high schools combined to form T. C. Williams High School.

1959 PTA letter
HAMMOND PARENT TEACHERS ASSOCIATION
Francis C. Hammond High School
Alexandria, Virginia
February 5, 1959

TO ALL PARENTS OF STUDENTS AT FRANCIS HAMMOND
HIGH SCHOOL

The Federal District Court has ordered the Alexandria School Board to admit two Negro students to Hammond High School no later than Tuesday, February 10, 1959.

Since its opening in September, 1956, Hammond High
School has established fine standards of scholarship,
sportsmanship, and citizenship. We expect to maintain
those standards.
We ask your help in this, as parents, by stressing the
Need for obedience to law, cooperation with the faculty, and an understand-
ing of other students.
We believe that the educational opportunities offered by Hammond High
School are as great as ever before and deserve the continued attendance of all
students now enrolled.

Sincerely yours,
EXECUTIVE COMMITTEE,
Francis Hammond High School
Parent-Teacher Association
By George W. Croker, President

As an aside, there was tremendous rivalry between Hammond, GW, and other high schools in Arlington and Fairfax Counties that would, periodically, feature semi approved vandalism. An eighteenth-century cannon was strategically placed at the intersection of Russell and Braddock Roads in Alexandria. Students living on the east side of Russell Road attended GW High School, and those living west of Russell Road went to Hammond. It seems that for years before or after football games, this poor piece of artillery would receive a vivid array of paint colors thrown from gallon sized buckets. No one would take responsibility, and no one was arrested for their creative work. These vibrant colors bedeviled the cannon for days before maintenance crews could clean the paint off the cannon and its stone base. Eventually, this prankster act would die out, and alas, the cannon has remained unpainted for years.

A discussion ensued one evening with Max, my best friend from Hammond High School, over the fate of the cannon. After an evening meal and libations at his country club, we decided to reestablish the long-lost tradition of dousing the cannon with colorful paint. Fortunately, we then decided it might be wiser to leave the cannon unscathed and returned to our homes. When I mentioned this improbable attack on the cannon to a former administrator with Alexandria city schools, he mentioned that we should have waited until 4:00 a.m. That was when the police shift changed. That way, we'd be less likely to be apprehended. Thank goodness cooler heads prevailed, and the infamous cannon escaped that terrible fate.

Growing up in an affluent community, I was fortunate to have access to good baseball stadiums in which our games were played. Simpson Field offered two playing fields, one for the Little League and a second for American Legion and high-school games. Hammond and GW had practice fields on their school properties. The Simpson fields were both fenced and lighted and had dugouts with running water. The stands were well situated, and there were public bathrooms and a concession stand.

In contrast, the field at Prince Edward County High School that was used by the All-Stars a few times during the summer did not have water in the dugouts, and there were no concession stands or bathroom facilities. The primary field used by the All-Stars was actually situated just over the county line in Cumberland County. Basically, there was a backstop and pitcher's mound

The cannon at Russell Road and Braddock Road awaits paint.

and not much else. There was no outfield fence, and there were mixed ground rules for fly balls to the outfield; such a ball was either a ground-rule double or a home run, depending on whether the ball landed in the brush or the woods. The infield was a combination of stones, dirt, and more stones, while the outfield had little in the way of grass. It was truly a fielder's nightmare.

Neighborhoods in both communities were, for the most part, segregated. African Americans predominantly lived in the Old Town area of Alexandria, while white families lived in the suburban area of the city boundaries. As the city became more gentrified, prices of homes in the Old Town area began to skyrocket, forcing many African American families to move to less pricey neighborhoods in Fairfax and Arlington Counties. Later, in the seventies and eighties, busing children to different schools in the city became an avenue to further integrate the schools. Less emphasis was placed on where children actually lived in order to more equally house students by race. In the early 1980s, I served as the principal of Charles Barrett Elementary School in Alexandria. The school's population hovered in the 350 range, with an almost-equal distribution of African American, Hispanic, Asian, and white students. Many students were bused to the school, and its rich diversity helped make it an outstanding school—a place where all children were loved, respected, and treated wonderfully by a professional and nurturing staff. It was one of my most favored educational experiences.

While the dropout rate was higher than desirable in Alexandria, the rate in Prince Edward County would become horrendous after the schools reopened in 1964. A huge number of the high-school students who had remained in Prince Edward County during the period of school closings chose not to return to school. Therefore, no diplomas would be forthcoming for them. Many felt too old to go back to earn a GED.

This directly affected the All-Stars, as many just gave up on education. In a few cases chronicled in the narratives section of this book, several players did not return to school. Of those that did, many felt ill prepared to attend college. What a colossal waste of intellect that, to this day, has lingering effects on the black and white communities. Some students were offered scholarships to college and refused them because they were too far behind due to the school closings. Several athletes couldn't play when the schools reopened due to their age. For some, it was especially devastating, as they could have had an opportunity to play sports in college or professionally, but they were denied that chance when their high-school careers were obliterated.

Growing up in Alexandria was a special treat, as the city offered unique and historic homes in which to live, surrounded by museums, theaters, professional sports teams, and numerous recreational opportunities. Yet Alexandria had its dark side too. I vividly remember going to the quaint train station only to find a separate section of the station house relegated to African Americans. There were signs over the entrance to the bathrooms stating For Colored Only and For Whites Only over the water fountain! My mother had a difficult time explaining what those signs meant.

Farmville, in contrast, was a quiet southern town with a smoldering cauldron of hatred and bigotry for the African American community. A friend of mine, another professor at Longwood College, told me that when he first arrived in Farmville to begin teaching a few years earlier, he saw a sign prominently placed on the road entering the town with the following message: WELCOME TO FARMVILLE…HOME OF THE KU KLUX KLAN! This was a chilling welcome for visitors as well as for the African American population that had to deal with that mentality on a daily basis. And as late as 1967, after fifteen years of playing baseball, I had not played with or against an African American player—not in Little League, not in Junior Major League, not in high school, not in American Legion play or at American University. In this instance, the differences were not so great.

Another huge logistical difference was the distance to fields for kids to be able to play ball. Kids in Alexandria either walked or rode their bikes to ball fields located throughout the city in public parks and on numerous high-school fields. My counterparts in Prince Edward were relegated to using the high-school field or one of the dirt fields, all devoid of any grass, that were scattered around the county. Obviously, most African American kids couldn't walk or bike to these fields, and consequently, they had to wait for parents or older siblings to drive them to practice or games.

Moving to Farmville to teach early-childhood education courses seemed a long way away from my earlier dream of playing professional baseball. Who would have thought that moving to this small rural community in southern Virginia would lead to a resurgence in my baseball career? Playing baseball for the All-Stars for three years and amassing a 22–1 pitching record would be the closest I would get to playing professional ball. While we didn't have wonderful uniforms; play on manicured, lighted fields; or travel across the country playing Major League opponents, we did enjoy playing before two hundred to three hundred fans per game with the belief that we were the best team in our place in the sun! And while we were not televised, local radio stations would occasionally broadcast our games, supplying endless cheer for so many who could not make it to the game.

With all the differences in cultural and educational opportunities and income availability, the overriding, single most unifying aspect between these two communities was the absolute love of the game of baseball. This thirty-plus-year-old white college professor would meet, join, and revere a varied collection of African American men and younger men who all cherished playing the national pastime. Differences in skin color, physical boundaries, and educational opportunities made no matter. The Farmville All-Stars, whose community was saddled with blatant bigotry, survived these atrocities through their faith and a bonding of families and friends that is still richly evident so many years later.

I could not have asked for a better baseball environment in which to end my career in Farmville. Few players ever have the opportunity of being so successful on a team of gifted athletes whose major desire was to play baseball for the Farmville All-Stars. Young boys would watch the All-Stars on game day and dream of playing for them in the future, reveling in becoming part of the legend. And thanks to the All-Stars, who expressed no bigotry to a white baseball player, I had the privilege of sharing my dream of playing the game we all truly loved with teammates who became dear and respected friends.

CHAPTER 7

Pitching

So how did I feel now that I had been accepted on the team? The last organized game of baseball I played had been in the spring of 1967. I pitched an inning in a reunion game at American University...and then nothing until that fateful day when I had a tryout for the All-Stars with Ricky Brown and Lorenzo Clark. Yes, I had a tryout to make sure I was good enough to play with the team. That was the rule, as the All-Stars had become a legend in south-side Virginia for their winning ways. One didn't just walk up and become a member. The tryout was just the first step. Once you were put on the team, you had to wait for a space to open in the position you wanted to play. In other words, if you wanted to play shortstop, you had to realize that position was Lorenzo's until he quit playing or you could beat him out of the spot. It was easier being a pitcher because more were needed for the regular weekend games. My wait for a spot in the rotation to play was quite brief. As I recall, I was able to start my first game for the All-Stars within two weeks of joining the club. After my first start, my pitching rotation was one day out of every weekend for the three years I played. I took a great deal of pride in my pitching and a greater amount of thanksgiving for the fantastic team with whom I was playing.

It took a while to even find my baseball glove that was packed away with other aging memorabilia from earlier days. It definitely needed to be cleaned and oiled before being put back in use. What relics my two gloves are today! The first, purchased in the early 1960s, is so worn that it is impossible to read the manufacturer's name. The second, a Regent 60 EZ Trap, would see me through high school, American Legion, and American University. Who would have thought it would be called upon again in the mid-1970s to once more perform its primary function of catching batted or thrown balls?

I had established, years earlier, a routine for preparation for each game. In high school and college, I was used primarily as a starting pitcher. In that role, I focused on each batter and their place in the batting order. The first summer of American Legion competition found me coming off the bench to quell opposing teams. I knew that I'd be throwing fewer than nine innings, so I could count on using every bit of strength and guile to get batters out.

With the All-Stars, I knew my role would be that of a starter. We played nine-inning games, so I had to conserve my energy in order to complete each game. My repertoire included a curve ball, knuckleball, and—lo and behold—a fastball. After college, I gained weight and swelled to 190 pounds. Perhaps it was just my mind, but I did feel that my fastball had increased in velocity. My efforts years ago throwing against the brick wall at my family home paid off. My control of throwing to the strike zone or wherever the catcher wanted made me a much more effective pitcher and allowed me to last for a nine-inning game.

I mentally prepared for each game well before game time. For the most part, I knew we were going to play men of all sizes and abilities. There would be a good selection of savvy baseball veterans who could really rip the ball. They would have to be carefully assessed and pitched around. There were other players who had natural abilities with less power. These, too, would undergo the same scrutiny. Occasionally, we'd face a few opposing batters who were there to fill up the roster. Each of these categories of batters could hit the ball with varying degrees of success.

Fortunately, my control and command of the strike zone proved to be fruitful. Many of the better opposing batters knew how to crush a fastball, as that was the most consistent pitch thrown in this south-side Virginia league. In my three seasons with the All-Stars, there were few who had mastered the curve and even fewer, if any, who had an effective knuckleball. My increased weight, the ability to hit the catcher's glove, and the curve and knuckleball all helped me be successful as an All-Star.

The All-Stars were blessed to have Ricky Brown and Les Hall as their main catchers. Both were tall, athletic, powerful hitters and were knowledgeable about a batter's weaknesses. They could determine if a batter would be susceptible to a curve ball or could hit the long ball by the way he stood in the batter's box. They could distract the batter with idle chatter or convince the hitter that he didn't have a chance getting on base. And they both had strong and accurate throws to second base to nail runners attempting to steal a base.

I was fortunate to have Ricky and Les behind the plate. They were masters at moving the target around the plate in an effort to fool the batter. Forty years later, both are paying the price, as their knees took such a beating catching so many games.

The All-Stars won many games due to players such as these, including Lorenzo "Hot Dog" Clark, Sally Robinson, Will and Anthony Robinson, William "Sheepdog" Johnson, Edward Thornton, Walter Brown, Samuel "Bug" Gilliam, Willie Blanton, and so many more. We were successful due to excellent fielding on less-than-stellar fields and batters who could consistently drive in runs. I was blessed to pitch for a team that was defensively superior and offensively gifted. No matter how many runs I gave up pitching in a game, the All-Stars would rise to the occasion and drive in as many runs as were needed to win!

My dad was happy that I was pitching again. I think he took pleasure in my phone calls to him describing the game I had just pitched. He was pleased and a little surprised that I had such a winning streak. He drove down from Alexandria to Farmville to see a game, which we won by five or six runs. My father's first comment after the game was "It's a good thing your team drives in so many runs!" And he was right!

Other than my pitching, I think I shocked my teammates by my ability to get on base either by a walk or hit, and my ability to steal bases. White pitchers are not known for their batting prowess, let alone their base stealing. In my midthirties, I amazed myself by getting on base a majority of my at-bat opportunities. Once on base, I utilized the good training from previous coaches and stole several bases during my three-year career with the All-Stars. I do remember laughter and amazement from my teammates as I'd steal another base. I was awash in good feelings from them and thrived on their natural banter over the "white guy."

Those were heady times for me, until I lost my last game pitching for the All-Stars. A good team from Maryland came south to play us, and I was just outplayed. Mercifully, I was pulled from the game by Boo, the coach. What a terrible way to end my career with the All-Stars. After twenty-two straight wins, I was tagged with the loss. And yet, I have thousands of marvelous memories playing three years with a great team. We started off as teammates and eventually became good friends. How bad could that be?

Warming up before the game or before the start of each inning allowed me to be clandestine in my delivery and effectiveness. I would never throw hard or throw a specialty pitch, such as a knuckleball. Warm-up pitches were vanilla throws to the plate. I wanted to mask what the batters were going to see when they stepped up to the plate. These pitches were just an opportunity to loosen my arm for the rigors of the impending inning. I would also consider their place in the batting order, knowing that the ninth player can sometimes hurt you as much as the first four to five batters in the order.

I would size up each batter as they stepped up to the plate, looking at the way they carried themselves, their height and weight, and whether or not they had the Look. Really solid players knew how to project the Look, and those who had it would receive special consideration in the pitches they would see. The defining attribute of my success was the simple fact that each of the All-Stars had the Look, whether or not they knew it. They just projected the Look when arriving for a game, when warming up, and before the game started, and the opposing team knew they were in trouble. The Look had helped seal the victory before the game had even started. Ricky Brown, the primary catcher who had the Look, tells the story of the All-Stars scoring thirteen runs in the first inning of one game. Several players went to Boo Jackson, the coach, recommending that the infrequently players get a chance to play. This would allow those first stringers coming out of the game to visit a small tavern adjacent to the field. Obviously, a good time was had by all that day!

At the 2015 reunion, I could still see the Look throughout the assembled All-Stars. The Look lives on in the guys forty years later…a tribute to the basic belief in themselves and their teammates. While death has claimed many of our teammates, those remaining still carry themselves as champions. My mind still sees these aging athletes suiting up for one more game on a glorious weekend, bolstered by an adoring crowd and the respect of an opposing team.

CHAPTER 8
Sandlot Baseball

BASEBALL IS SUCH A SIMPLE game, yet so complex. It's elegant but dirty. There's grand joy when a pitcher hits the right corner of the plate for a strike and utter defeat when a fielder misplays a grounder or a long fly ball. To each player there are joys and pains on every pitch. Each one is more important than the last. Games can be won or lost on one pitch. Forty years ago, national statistics showed that if a batter walked, there was an 85 percent probability that he would eventually score. I don't believe that figure is much different today.

Most pitchers have two or three pitches at their command: fastball, off speed, curve, slider, cutter, knuckleball, and so on. Many have true command of one or two. Few can be proficient at all, and those that do are feared by the batter.

Eye-hand coordination for a batter is absolutely necessary to be successful. Batters have a precious second to decide whether to swing at a pitch or to back off and not swing. Players who miss 70 percent of the pitches thrown to them become feared among their competitors. Professionally, they can command high salaries. It's hard to fathom how a batter with a 30 percent success rate can earn millions of dollars in salary and incentives. It seems that at every level these statistics are valid, whether one is looking at Little League or Major League players.

Many of the ball fields we played at were high-school sites or fields in the country generally within fifty miles of Farmville. They ranged from good grass infields and outfields to less-than-adequate playing surfaces. The home team supplied bases and home plate. At some ballparks there were no stands, and people stood for the game. Dugouts ran the gamut of brick or concrete enclosed structures to a single board nailed to four-by-fours. It just didn't matter to the All-Stars, nor did it matter to our opponents. We were there to play ball. The ball bounced crazily for either team. Some stadiums had outfield fences. Sometimes Lorenzo, Les, and Ricky hit the ball so far the outfielders couldn't catch up to it! One time I was pitching in AltaVista, Virginia, when a batter smacked a knuckleball to center field. Because there were no outfield fences, our center fielder Bug Gilliam was able to haul it in. Our outfielders saved me in so many games with their fielding abilities.

Running water was generally not available unless we played at a high-school stadium, and even then, the water was generally cut off. Heavy-duty coolers seemed to predominate. Sucking on lemons, a tactic taught by Ray Struder, my Post 24 coach from Alexandria, helped immensely during those hot, steamy summers in Virginia.

There were backstops at each field, which was helpful. While there were also pitching mounds at each field, they varied in degree from good to barely functional. You just adapted. Umpires were provided by the home team. They all did a fairly good job of calling balls, strikes, and outs. It was not a job for the weak of heart as, generally, there was only one umpire. And there was no instant replay!.

Fans enjoying game at Cumberland Field.

CHAPTER 9

All-Star Fans

THE LOCAL COMMUNITIES WOULD TURN out with varying degrees of enthusiasm and size. It was not uncommon for the All-Stars to attract crowds of up to three hundred people, including families, friends, wives, girlfriends, and lovers of the game. It was a social gathering for all. I'm sure some never watched the game, as they were tending to children or talking with friends.

During my years with the All-Stars, there were no negative incidents involving the fans. Baseball was paramount, and the All-Stars always seemed to win. There were times of heated discussions, but no punches were thrown, and games were played with intensity and zeal. Many fans knew baseball well and were appreciative of the high level of ball played by the All-Stars.

After one game in which I pitched fairly well in a tight All-Star win, a fan came up and said, "You pitched a good game."

I replied, "Yes, I did. Thanks."

The fan looked surprised by my comment and walked away muttering to himself. I learned from that encounter to control my feelings and deflect positive comments to my teammates, who continually made me look good through their hitting and fielding. I used this exchange as an example in my classes at Longwood College and at numerous early-childhood education national conferences to help people realize that most people prefer humility rather than acknowledging and accepting praise. I wasn't trying to be bombastic to the person who complimented me, just recognizing a job well done.

Again, I learned from that encounter to deflect positive comments to the team, whether it be in baseball, the classroom, or life in general. I also believe that some people will deny that they have done a good job when complimented just to have the person repeat their praise, because the denier had such a low self-concept that they wanted to hear the person repeat his compliment. A sad commentary!

It was definitely a social gathering on the weekends. Fans and families looked forward to weekends filled with outstanding baseball. For many in south-side Virginia, these games were the highlight for social activities for many in the African American community. Wives, girlfriends, and fans followed the All-Stars to their home field in Cumberland County just north of Farmville. Fans also traveled to away games as far as sixty to seventy miles from Farmville. In the twenty-plus years of the All-Stars' existence, there were no major traffic accidents or incidents involving safety to fans or players. Many of the wives would plan for food preparation for the games, from grilling hot dogs and hamburgers to baking cakes and pies. Needless to say, beer and other libations were also available!

On away games, our fans were always well treated by the home team's fans. I was amazed to hear how many players and wives were related to other players. It is my guess that many fans from both the home team and the visitors were related. The rivalries among the teams were highlighted by the fact that so many were related.

During the seventies, one of the local radio stations in Farmville would occasionally broadcast the game. For those who couldn't attend the games, this was a tremendous way to stay in touch with the All-Stars. After the games ended, I wasn't a white guy standing out in an all-black fan base. I was an All-Star, a ballplayer and lover of the game. I do believe that fans came to realize that for at least a few hours each weekend, we weren't black or white…just a group of people mixing and mingling to enjoy the national pastime together in a community where there wasn't much in the way of positive interchanges in the sixties and seventies.

CHAPTER 10

Picnics, Parties, and Reunions

THROUGHOUT THE YEARS I PLAYED with the All-Stars, 1976–78, we had parties and picnics at my 1821 farmhouse near Sailor's Creek Battlefield, site of the last battle of the Civil War. We all enjoyed each other's company at these functions that included players, wives, girlfriends, and fans. At other times, the All-Stars were invited to my home for open-house parties. I marveled at the affairs held at my home. At various summer parties at my home in the country, we enjoyed roasting pigs and watching movies in the evening on a sheet hanging outside of the second-floor bedroom, while people were seated in lawn chairs, stretched out on blankets, or just standing around enjoying the company. At one of the parties, ballplayers and other guests tried to ride one of my horses. All who tried were unceremoniously brushed off by tree branches and fell to the ground. My horse, Daiquiri, a beautiful palomino, loved to brush off unsuspecting riders with the low-hanging black walnut tree branches.

Watching the joy of these events was tempered by the fact that 150 years earlier, slaves tended to the house and fields. At least now, my farm was a place of comfort and joy for a segment of the African American community that had been so terribly mistreated by so many in Prince Edward County.

Many reunions have been held over the years. My wife, Mo, and I have attended a few with great joy. It's amazing to me that after so many years, the remaining All-Stars still revel in each other's company. It's as if one large

This was my home, The Farmer House, a Virginia state Landmark.

family, split by distance and circumstance, comes together to enjoy each other again. So many told me they would love to suit up for one more game. The will and desire to persevere remains constant in these men—from Gilbert Scott, one of the oldest players, to Sam Sims, one of the youngest. If you played for the All-Stars, you remain an All-Star. These reunions are punctuated by laughter and stories of past victories, and children and grandchildren sit around listening to the exploits of the players, recognizing that many of the stories may be embellished. The All-Stars put aside hatred and animosity to accept me and, later, other white players into their select few, believing, "It's not just black or white!"

1996 All Stars Reunion

2015 All Stars Reunion

Narratives

⁓

COMPILED BY THE AUTHOR AFTER *each player completed a questionnaire and/or interview.*

WILLIE BLANTON

Willie played for the All-Stars from 1967 to 1972 and again from 1976 to 1980. He played ball for Luther P. Jackson High School as an outfielder and first baseman in 1967 and 1968. In his senior year, Willie was voted as the most valuable player.

Willie stated that he didn't have any particular feelings about a white man joining the team. One of his best friends while growing up near the Old Lipscomb Store in Cumberland County was Jerry Rousey. Together, they played daily during summer vacation, including wonderful games of "sock ball" (played with a baseball-sized rock encased in a sock). Willie wrote that "in spite of being different, we were alike in many ways." They attended segregated schools but continued being friends before they eventually went their different ways. Willie felt that Jerry helped him interact with people throughout his life. During his years with the All-Stars, he saw that the team continued their winning ways with the addition of white players, especially pitchers. "The guys were very talented, but also very likable guys."

One of his fondest memories with the All-Stars took place when Willie, as a teenage player, traveled with the team to Newark, New Jersey, in the summer of 1967, to play the Newark Tigers. He only came to bat once and saw three pitches, all fastballs for strikes, but he was thrilled to have been in the game. He also enjoyed playing against the team from Keysville, our fiercest competitor. Many of the games were broadcast over radio stations in Farmville. Not your normal coverage in south-side Virginia! Willie remembers hitting many home runs, especially one in Buckingham County. He recalls a potential home run that an opposing player hit into the outfield. Since many of the fields did not have fences, it was questionable whether a batted ball was a home run or a ground-rule double. On at least one occasion, a ball was hit into the left-field tree line. Willie got to the ball and threw it to Lorenzo, whose throw to the plate cut the runner down. So an apparent home run was turned into an out. "Most of all, it was a time of great fellowship with a great group of guys and wonderful fans."

Willie earned two graduate degrees, one in education (MEd) and the other in public administration (MPA). He was a teacher at a Virginia correctional center and also taught community college courses as an adjunct instructor. Willie pursued a doctorate in public administration from Virginia Tech and completed his residency but had to drop out due to the rigors of raising a growing family. His work experience includes serving as a department head with the City of Charlottesville and as director of workforce development for the Commonwealth of Virginia, as well as working for the Virginia Employment Commission and the Virginia Community College System. He retired from the commonwealth with thirty-two years of service. He's a father of three children, and now he's known as PaPa, having one grandchild. Quite a remarkable individual!

On the questionnaire that each All-Star completed, Willie summed it all up by adding, "Boo was the glue! Lorenzo was the star! The rest of us were just great support cast."

Willie Blanton

CLYDE BROWN

Clyde was initially a pitcher but took over duties as the manager/coach of the team for two years in the 1970s. He also played in France when he was in the service. He enjoyed coaching the Robinson brothers, Will and Anthony, describing them as good players. Clyde took advantage of the GI Bill and became a certified plumber. He engaged in that profession until his retirement. For a time, Clyde enjoyed raising pigs. He is now retired and enjoys living in the Farmville/Cumberland area.

Clyde Brown

RICKY BROWN

Ricky played with the All-Stars as a catcher from 1972 to 1986. During this writer's three years with the All-Stars, Ricky was the primary catcher for the team. He grew up in downtown Farmville and was greatly affected by the 1959–64 school closings. Ricky came from a family of ten children and consequently missed all five years of school during the closings. He had minimal educational opportunities during those years, learning only the alphabet and how to spell his name. He did play baseball, football, and basketball for Prince Edward County High School after the schools reopened.

Ricky tells a funny, yet sad story about venturing into the Leggett's department store at the tender age of five and promptly getting on the elevator by himself. Not knowing how to read or write, he started pushing buttons as the door closed and the elevator began its ascent. Alarmed, Ricky started pushing all the buttons, eventually hitting the stop button. To his consternation, the elevator stopped between floors. Store employees finally were able to free Ricky from the elevator. The story is humorous now, but the experience must have been frightening for a young boy.

It didn't bother Ricky to have a white man join the team. He was only concerned that the guy could pitch. One of his fondest memories of the All-Stars was an inside-the-park homerun at Parker Field (the Diamond), which was home then to the AAA farm team for the Atlanta Braves. This was quite a feat, as Ricky was not the fleetest player on the team.

Instilling pride and a sense of accomplishment were easy tasks for him. He was an imposing player that the whole team looked to for leadership and support. Ricky made everyone laugh with his sense of humor and helped reinforce the idea that no team could beat the All-Stars. Boo, the team's manager for many years, would cajole Ricky to go out to the mound and tell the pitcher what to do. In the writer's case, I was ten years older, had two graduate degrees, and pitched for American University. When Ricky came out to calm me down or make a suggestion for a certain pitch, I'd just say, "Yes, sir!" He instinctually knew what the pitcher could do and what the batter couldn't. He was a gifted player and is a dear friend.

Ricky Brown

WALTER BROWN

Walter played for the All-Stars in the seventies and coached the team in the eighties. He played baseball for Luther Jackson High School in Cumberland County as a pitcher and right fielder. During his term of duty in the army, he played right field and pitched on a service team in Germany. He mentioned that there were good players and some professional players scattered throughout the country playing for their respective camps.

Due to the school closings, Walter moved to Cumberland to live with his grandfather. His brother, Ricky, was younger and stayed in Farmville with his mother, not going to school until the schools reopened in 1964. Walter was not bothered by a white man joining the team. He told me that I was the first white player for the All-Stars. In subsequent years, other white players joined the team. Efforts are underway to determine if the author was the first white player in the league.

Walter enjoyed being around a good bunch of guys who also happened to be good team players. His fondest memories included being around the fans who traveled throughout south-side Virginia following the team. The atmosphere after the games was always relaxed and enjoyable.

Walter recently retired from Hampden-Sydney College in Worsham, Virginia, where he was the special projects manager for the school.

Walter Brown

ROBERT LEWIS CARTER

Robert had lived in Prince Edward and Cumberland Counties all of his life. During the years the All-Stars played baseball, Robert Lewis and another volunteer, Pee Wee, collected gate receipts from the fans who attended the games. A fee was collected as carloads of fans from both teams arrived, with the money being turned over to the coach/manager, Boo Jackson. Since the ballplayers were not charged a fee, they were not involved in money transactions. No one really challenged Boo about funds collected from the fans. Ricky and I thought there might be a fee of one dollar per person, but Robert Lewis said that the fee was three dollars per person. The team the All-Stars played and the location of the game had an effect on the total amount collected. Robert Lewis said he thought the highest gate was in the range of $700–$800. This was a significant amount of money, and there was always money available for balls, bats, and uniforms. After the game, there was plenty to eat and drink, paid for through gate receipts.

Robert Lewis worked for the Town of Farmville for a number of years. Gerald Spates, the Farmville town manager, said he couldn't do his job without Robert Lewis. He was viewed as a trusted employee by the town government.

His parting words to Ricky Brown and me were prophetic: "I never took a penny." The money was always turned over to Boo Jackson, who took care of making sure there were sufficient funds available for supplies. Robert Lewis Carter's quiet demeanor helps one believe that no truer words were ever spoken!

The author is sad to report that Robert Lewis Carter passed away after the All-Star reunion was held in September 2015. The author sat next to Robert Lewis and enjoyed his company and fellowship at the reunion. His loss will be great for all who knew him.

Robert Lewis Carter

Lorenzo "Hot Dog" Clark

Lorenzo played with the All-Stars from the mid-1960s to the mid-1980s. He was quite young when he started and was therefore placed at second base so he wouldn't have to throw the ball too far. He used his first glove for seven or eight years after it had been donated to the team along with balls, bats, and gloves by W. A. Reid, a local businessman. During the school closing, Lorenzo attended local churches where volunteer teachers helped students as much as they could under very trying conditions. When the school system did reopen, Lorenzo played for the high-school baseball team; however, he could not play his senior year due to his age.

He was drafted by the Baltimore Orioles and was later traded to the Washington Senators and played in their rookie league in Bluefield, West Virginia. He dislocated an ankle, which kept him out of the game for five weeks of rehabilitation. Lorenzo then was sent to Lewiston, Utah, where he played every day at second base, third base, and shortstop. That winter he played in Opa-locka, Florida, concentrating on third base and short-stop. In his long career with the All-Stars, Lorenzo excelled at shortstop while also pitching and catching.

Hot Dog was not bothered by a white man joining the team. He stated that he didn't look at color. His fondest memories included playing at Parker Field, the Diamond, in Richmond, Virginia. This was the home stadium for the AAA ball club of the Atlanta Braves. He hit a home run in Richmond, which was a thrill for Lorenzo, although he hit home runs in every park the All-Stars played in. He was one of the most fluid players this writer has ever seen. He also enjoyed playing at Potter Field in Appomattox, Virginia.

Lorenzo has been married for over forty years. He worked for the sheriff's department and owns and operates a backhoe business. He's also worked in a funeral home. He feels blessed to have two grown daughters and one grand-child. While he still entertains desires to continue playing, his body is not up to the task, even when his mind says "Go." After the eighties, he played softball with many of the older All-Stars in Richmond, Virginia, and other localities in surrounding counties.

There were countless memories of playing with the All-Stars. Hot Dog thoroughly enjoyed playing with the guys as they grew up together playing ball.

I remember a dance at the National Guard Armory in Farmville where I was the only white person in attendance. A fight broke out, and almost immediately, several of the All-Stars surrounded me for protection. Hot Dog told me to put my hand on his waist and not to worry. As I did, I felt a gun at his waist. I asked how many guns there were in the armory, and Lorenzo replied, "You don't want to know!" I will state that as a deputy sheriff, Lorenzo had the right to carry a gun.

Currently, one of Lorenzo's daughters is running for the commonwealth attorney's position in Prince Edward County, which is an exciting event for his whole family and the All-Star family.

PS: Megan Clark was elected in November 2015 to serve as the first African American commonwealth's attorney for Prince Edward County!

Lorenzo Clark

SAMUEL "BUG" GILLIAM

Bug played quite a long time for the All-Stars, from 1960 to 1976. He originally played with the Cumberland Sluggers. He was versatile enough to play third base, shortstop, and center field. Bug grew up in Cumberland County and therefore was not affected by the school closings in Prince Edward County. He indicated it was fine with him for a white man to join the team; the first for the All-Stars was Aubry. Bug was somewhat withdrawn from Aubry for the first few games, not saying much to him. Aubry was pitching one Sunday at the Prince Edward High School field and was being verbally harassed by the opposing team and their fans. After a few innings of this abuse, Bug grabbed a bat and walked over to the visitors' dugout and stands. In clear and loud terms, Bug told the team and fans to leave Aubry alone as he was a member of the All-Stars and anybody who didn't would have to deal with Bug! The stands and dugout grew quiet for the rest of the game, and Aubry knew he had finally been accepted as a teammate.

Bug enjoyed playing ball for the All-Stars and especially liked the post-game social activities of having a few beers while discussing the game with friends. He went on to play softball with members of the All-Stars throughout central Virginia.

Samuel has been retired for the last seven years. He has taken up the game of golf and is now shooting in the eighties, very respectful scores!

Samuel 'Bug' Gilliam

Les Hall

Les's fondest memories of the All-Stars were winning, making friends, and being with the team. He played first base and catcher. Les played hard-pitch softball while he was in the air force in Tucson, South Vietnam, and Langley, Virginia. He worked for the Post Office, retiring after twenty-two years of service. It didn't bother Les about a white man joining the All-Stars. He had been a minority on the softball team in the service. Les would practice throwing the ball at the barracks wall to help develop his accuracy. He had a heartfelt desire to play at the Diamond field in Richmond, then home of the AAA farm team of the Atlanta Braves.

Les enjoyed the party atmosphere after the games. He would comment tongue in cheek that by the third inning, he would have had three beers! He felt that the All-Stars were always ready to play and the caliber of the players was so superior to that of their opponents. Les always enjoyed hitting home runs, especially he and Sally, now deceased, down Griffin Street. His favorite site, though, was the Diamond, "where the left field wall kept calling" for him.

His years of catching did wreak havoc on his knees, causing him some pain and discomfort. Les seemed larger than life at times, especially when he'd ride his motorcycle to the game in his uniform! His wit and sense of humor do, though, persist! Thank God.

Les Hall

JAMES HOLCOMB

Jim was a member of the All-Stars from 1965 to 1973. He primarily played with a team from Darlington Heights and for Virginia State University. During a previous stay in Maryland, he attended a tryout promoted by the Pittsburgh Pirates at the University of Maryland. Jim had no problem with a white man joining the team and would have enjoyed it. He was especially pleased with the togetherness of the team. He focused his energy on playing center field.

For the past thirty-plus years, Jim taught health and physical education and driver's education for Prince Edward County High School. He also served as the athletic director and assistant principal at the high school. James felt that the All-Stars were a special group of ballplayers, and he enjoyed being a part of the team.

WILLIAM "SHEEPDOG" JOHNSON

Sheepdog played for the All-Stars from 1976 to 1980. He was a first baseman the entire time he played. He also played for the Prince Edward Sheriff's Department and the Richmond UFOs. William started school in 1964, the year the schools reopened, and was not affected by the closing.

Sheep was cool with a white player joining the team as long as we treated each other as people. He liked the way everyone, on and off the team, treated people as family.

He's been active in the community for the last thirty-five years and played softball up until the last fifteen years. William married Janice Allen and joined Race Baptist Church in 1992. For the past thirteen years, he has served as a deacon at the church. He owns and operates a concrete company servicing the town of Farmville and Prince Edward County.

The team has held reunions at William's home. He has always enjoyed the family atmosphere among the All-Stars. It doesn't matter that the All-Stars haven't played in thirty years...we all belong to a brotherhood that exists to this day.

William 'SheepDog' Johnson

Hilton Lee

Hilton's tenure with the All-Stars lasted from 1974 to 1985. He played right field and loved every minute of it. When the schools closed, Hilton would have been in the sixth grade. He never returned to school for a formal education. He felt that the school closings had a worse effect on the white population of Prince Edward County. In a discussion with a white woman who asked him if he was upset with losing those years with no education, Hilton replied, "It hurt you more than it hurt me. You have to count on me and others who were hurt by the closing of schools. Who's going to fix your plumbing, car, heating, and air conditioning and take care of you when you age?"

Hilton has a strong belief in Jesus Christ and has turned his life over to Jesus to help him through the difficult times. Ricky Brown added during this conversation that "the schools closing were meant to happen here in Prince Edward because God knew the response from the African American community would be without violence." Their religious beliefs helped the All-Stars and many in the community to shoulder and deal with the pain and loss of education.

A white man joining the all-black team wasn't a problem for Hilton. He noted that "Aubry treated me as a man, and that's the way I treated him. The guy was quiet and easygoing, and that helped him be accepted by the team. And he could win and enjoyed a beer or two after the game too!" Aubry replied that "playing with the All-Stars was my equivalent to playing professional ball over a three-year period."

Hilton and Gilbert Scott related a hilarious story about Chester, manager of the Keysville Braves, a neighboring ball club that happened to be our fiercest competitor. Chester evidently complained that when Aubry was added to the All-Star roster, they were over the limit. That issue was quickly overcome as Chester was known for "bringing in new talent" for the day his team was scheduled to play the All-Stars.

The rivalry between the All-Stars and the Keysville team was legendary. During an interview session, a story unfolded about the All-Stars coming to Keysville to play the Keysville Braves. Managers Boo Jackson of Farmville and Chester Gregory of Keysville discussed the ground rules prior to the game, as there were no fences to determine the limits of the outfield. During the first inning, an All-Star hit a ball deep into the branches and bushes. Boo and Chester got into a huge argument over which was the correct call, a home run or a ground-rule double. The discussion became so heated that Boo told the All-Stars to "pack up their stuff" and head home. Much to the consternation of the paying crowd, the game ended. People were calling for the return of their money as the All-Stars left. Eventually, the state police had to be called. The trooper sent everyone home! Hilton and Gilbert recalled this fiasco with much laughter and merriment.

Hilton remembers so many good times with the All-Stars, but playing in Falls Church, Virginia, a suburb of Washington, DC, was a highlight for him. He said that his nickname was "Silk" because he was so smooth operating heavy construction equipment. He noted that most of the ballplayers were church members. He professes that God was his anchor both during the lost years of education in the school-closing period and during his later years as an adult in the heavy machinery business. According to Hilton, "We was bad" (the All-Stars). He told the writer that while God loved all players, he loved the All-Stars the most!

Hilton and many other African Americans of the early 1960s in Prince Edward County lost five critical years. Their educational base was dismantled, and county- and statewide athletics and cultural events were nonexistent for these students. Much was lost and never recovered from this five-year loss of their right to a quality education. It was truly disgraceful.

Hilton Lee

WILL ROBINSON

Will played with the All-Stars from 1970 to 1972 and 1976 to 1979. He also starred with Luther P. Jackson High School in Cumberland, Virginia, and Mansfield College in Pennsylvania. At Luther P. Jackson High School, he was a three-sport standout in football, basketball, and baseball. Will also was the captain of these sports in his senior year. Since he lived in Cumberland County, he was not affected by the school closings in Prince Edward County.

He was a teenager when the first white man joined the All-Stars, and he had no problem with it. He found it odd at the time because of the racial tension, past and present. It also served as a teaching tool for him as the men whom he held in high regard believed that the color of one's skin did not matter. Some of his fondest memories involved the level of play of the older players. While with the All-Stars, he pitched and played first base and outfield. Will felt honored to play with Lorenzo "Hot Dog" Clark, Bill Thornton, Ricky Brown, and Sam "Bug" Gilliam.

After graduating from Mansfield College, Will joined the staff at Luther P. Jackson High School as an assistant coach. Upon returning from a break from education, he returned to Cumberland as the head coach and guided them to three state tournament berths. Will then accepted the position of assistant coach at Robinson High School, in Fairfax County, Virginia. He then moved to be the assistant coach of the women's basketball program at George Mason University in Fairfax County, Virginia.

In 1987, Will became the head coach at Woodbridge Senior High School in Prince William County, Virginia. He led the team to over three hundred victories, which still stands as the most wins in the school's history. He later moved to Charlotte, North Carolina, to serve as the head coach of Vance High School. He reached a milestone at Vance by winning his five hundredth game. Will still holds the record for most wins at Vance High School! Will is unique in that he holds the most wins in two different high schools in two different states.

Some of his accomplishments include an overall coaching record of 525–170, thirteen district conference titles, fourteen regular-season titles, and four regular titles. He has been district coach of the year five times and has also been Virginia state coach of the year. He has conducted camps and clinics throughout the United States and abroad and has been a featured speaker at numerous camps and clinics. Will retired after thirty-six years of teaching and coaching and is active in his church's activities.

Will Robinson

GILBERT SCOTT

Gilbert indicated that the All-Stars began in May 1960. He is the oldest living All-Star and played with them from 1960 to 1965. During that period, John Bracy was the manager. Gilbert also played with the Five Forks ball club in Prospect, Virginia. During his career, Gilbert played at shortstop and second base and pitched. When the schools closed in 1959, he went to work operating a bulldozer. And though he never completed high school, he had no problem with a white guy joining the team.

He enjoyed the festivities that took place after the games, as well as discussing the game, including both highlights and mistakes. There were a lot of family members on the team, including brothers-in-law and cousins. It was fun traveling to the different sites for the away games in places such as Clarksville, Keysville, Amherst, Brookneal, Cumberland, Buckingham, Amelia, Charlotte, and Pamplin. Gilbert's son, Gilbert Tyren, played with the All-Stars, along with the offspring of earlier players. Gilbert also commented that there was never any trouble at any of the games. Fights just didn't happen. People were there to enjoy "The Game." This writer feels it must have been wonderful for Gilbert to see his son playing with the All-Stars.

Gilbert recalled that the trip to New Jersey to play a team there was quite an event. Everyone loved the enjoyment of a long trip with teammates whom one respected and enjoyed as friends. The long drive to New Jersey certainly helped cement positive feelings among the players.

[Gilbert Scott]

Sam Sims

Sam played with the All-Stars from 1980 to the team's final season in 1986. Prior to the All-Stars, he played for the Rice Tigers, a Little League team in the Farmville area. He was a pitcher for the All-Stars and was fond of the fact that he never lost a game while on the team. In addition to pitching, Sam also caught and played second base.

Sam was employed for the last thirty-plus years until his health failed. He loved playing for the All-Stars and couldn't wait for the next game to start.

Sam Sims

ROB STANLEY

Rob played two years with the All-Stars from 1978 to 1979. He played catcher and loved having Lorenzo Clark pitch so he could catch his fastball, which was legendary. He attended Prince Edward Academy, where he was a pitcher and catcher. He was a three-time all-conference catcher and was an all-conference pitcher in his senior year.

He loved playing ball with the All-Stars, as he knew many of them personally. It didn't bother him to be one of the few white men on the team. Rob felt accepted by the team and fans. He recalls one game when one of the fans was particularly hostile to him. When Rob had a tough tag at the plate of a runner attempting to score, he held his ground and flipped the runner completely over, tagging him out in the process. The verbal fan ceased his harassment after that tag.

Rob always felt at home playing with the All-Stars. One of his favorite moments with the team came when he was the catcher at Parker Field, then home of the AAA Richmond Braves. He states, "I really loved playing with those guys, especially Lorenzo and Down Town Ricky Brown. They could play the game and really challenged you every day to play as hard as they did. Always motivating, always positive, and always had your back! I still love talking with them today about the team."

Rob graduated with a BA in business from Randolph-Macon College in Ashland, Virginia, and a MEd from Ashland University in Ashland, Ohio. For a number of years, he coached football at such institutions as Patrick Henry High School in Ashland, Virginia; Ferrum Junior College in Ferrum, Virginia; Randolph-Macon College; Ashland University; and Virginia Military Institute in Lexington, Virginia.

His football exploits include being selected as the team captain at Prince Edward Academy, as well as most valuable player of the team and region. He was most valuable player of the East Bowl while at Ferrum Junior College and was all-conference linebacker and defensive captain at Randolph-Macon College.

In addition to his coaching activities, Rob has spent seventeen years in investment and insurance sales.

Rob Stanley

Edward "Carew" Thornton

Edward played with the Farmville All-Stars from 1967 to 1976. His baseball career began at Cumberland High School, and he also played at Virginia State University. He later took up softball in a Richmond league. He's currently a 4.5 tennis player who plays regularly.

He missed the first two years of school due to the closing of the schools in Prince Edward County. He attended school in Cumberland County for two years before returning to Prince Edward County High School, where he played baseball.

Edward passed up a scholarship to a prestigious local private men's college. He felt the early years he missed due to the schools closing impinged on his ability to be successful. The fear of failing struck such a dissonant chord for so many students.

He had no problem having a white player join the team, feeling that baseball had no color and the white guy (Aubry) could pitch and help the All-Stars win! A second baseman, Edward, vividly remembers hitting a home run at the Appomattox field.

"It was a pleasure playing with the guys because a lot of us started playing Little League, Pony League, and high school together," which created everlasting friendships. He tells the chilling story, though, of helping neighbors bale and pick up hay one day. That night his family noticed a blaze through the trees at their neighbors'. Rushing over to help, they witnessed a cross burning, complete with men wearing the traditional Ku Klux Klan robes. What a sight to see after having helped the farmer earlier in the day. Fortunately, Edward and his family were not seen by those attending the cross burning.

For the last thirty-five years, Edward has been working as an accountant. His athletic endeavors include softball, tennis, and golf. He's an accomplished musician playing drums.

Edward 'Carew' Thornton

SHIRBY SCOTT BROWN
WIFE OF RICKY BROWN

Shirby met Ricky Brown at Moton School, and they have been married for thirty-seven years. A native of adjoining Charlotte County, she was aware of the school closings in Prince Edward County. She graduated from Virginia State University in Petersburg, majoring in health and physical education. She taught seventh grade for thirty-four years before retiring.

She indicated that she didn't attend all the games, as she was caring for their young children at the time, and the distance involved in traveling to some of the games was too great. She is quite proud of Ricky's athletic abilities, stating that he was always open-minded and competitive. She especially admired his sportsmanship. Shirby felt Ricky had more raw talent than many professional ballplayers. She believed the All-Stars had great talent and were definitely head and shoulders ahead of other teams in the league.

Shirby's feelings for Ricky are so evident. She said he makes a difference in people's lives every day. She felt he was a "diamond in the rough" when she first met him. She introduced him to her parents, seven brothers and sisters, and her grandmother, and a bond was formed. In a community where it is hard for African Americans to gain respect, she says Ricky has done a great job of helping young men in the community find their way. Shirby said Ricky could meet and talk with a CEO or a wino, and that person's position wouldn't make a difference to him.

She just knows that he's respectful to her, adding, "We've built a great relationship, and he's respectful to me." It's obvious to this writer the love and caring these two share with each other.

Shirby was the first African American to serve as the athletic director for Prince Edward County High School, a huge distinction. In this position, she traveled to numerous state and regional meetings representing Prince Edward County.

Shirby Scott Brown

SHIRLEY BROWN
WIFE OF WALTER BROWN

Shirley grew up in a large baseball-oriented family in Prince Edward County. Her father was a baseball player who was scouted by the Brooklyn Dodgers as a possible professional player. Two of her brothers played for the All-Stars, and Boo Jackson, the coach/manager of the All-Stars, was her first cousin. To top it all off, Shirley met Walter Brown at a Farmville All-Stars game and thought he was good looking and interesting. Her niece, Charlotte, helped them meet, which has led to a wonderful forty-two years of marriage.

The school closings brought disaster to Shirley and her family. During the first year of closure, she attended school in Charlotte County, staying with family. She moved back to Prince Edward County the following year. She was able to receive some schooling in various church basements and rooms. She did attend the free school year in 1963. The situation was not good, as the schools were chaotic, with little administrative help and few supplies. It wasn't easy at all for Shirley and her classmates through those horrendous years. Families were split apart, and many children received little or no education during those five lost years. Even after the schools were reopened, it wasn't easy. Teachers had to be recruited and hired, supplies ordered, schools cleaned and refurbished, and children had to be placed as best as possible in the correct grade. Many families just didn't send their children back to school. So many years later, Shirley still can't believe it happened. She said some bitterness still lingers in the community. Her mother had to move three times within the Farmville community to help accommodate the needs of Longwood College's growth.

Shirley mentioned that everyone in the Farmville community loved the All-Stars. Each weekend brought people together to see the team play at a field just outside the city limits in Cumberland County or to travel to various other communities for the game. Many wives cooked at the games, providing fans and players with great home cooking, grilled hamburgers and hot dogs, and chilled beverages. The Farmville area loved the All-Stars. They took pride in the team, followed them throughout the state, and gathered together as friends and neighbors to cheer on their team. Wives, girlfriends, and lovers of baseball so looked forward to these games. The community felt special because the All-Stars were so special. The team enjoyed playing well and being respected by the fans and teams they played. It was as if the whole fan base was family with the team. And in many cases, it was! It was a remarkable feeling for the fans and the players.

Shirley Brown

Reitha Jackson
Wife of Deceased Manager/Coach Boo Jackson

Boo Jackson, the manager/coach of the All-Stars from 1963 to 1982, passed away on April 21, 2010. He also played first base while he coached. Reitha was glad to be included in the interview process, as she developed close relationships with the wives and players on the team. Some of her fondest memories included traveling with the team to the games. She mentioned that it was a very social time for the ladies, who would cook on portable grills and sell their food products. She misses the social interactions with the wives, girlfriends, and players.

She told an amusing story about when Aubry first joined the All-Stars. When Chester Gregory, the manager of the fierce rival Keysville Braves, found out a white man joined the All-Stars as a pitcher, he complained mightily, saying that the roster was set and Aubry should not be allowed to play. Boo Jackson obviously disregarded this request.

In addition, Reitha spoke about some of the fans who mentioned that a white man had joined the All-Stars as a pitcher. They were saying that he should not have been on the team. Nevertheless, Boo disregarded these comments and told them, "Color don't matter as long as he can pitch and play the game."

Reitha said the team carried itself well, arriving at the game site knowing that they were going to win before the game began. The opposing teams knew it too. The All-Stars couldn't lose and rarely did.

Reitha Jackson

JERRY SMITH
FAN AND UMPIRE

During the time of the school closings, Jerry was encouraged to read everything he could. He loved to read and discovered that Branch Café was a place where he could find solace in a book. In 1963, when the free school opened, there was mass confusion. Attempts were made to place children in appropriate grade-level classrooms with little success. People were held back while others were promoted a grade or two. Everybody's story was different. Kids were excited about the schools possibly reopening. It wasn't the young people who were hurt the most; it was the white generation that counted on the African American community to help in their homes and businesses that suffered the most.

Jerry enjoyed going to the games for the social atmosphere. Lots of people congregated from both teams, but there never was a fight, and the police never had to be called. He saw no color issue when Aubry became a member of the team. Jerry worked for the local A&P grocery store and was the only African American employee, so "sticking out" was not a matter of concern to him.

He later worked at a convenience store after the A&P closed. Jerry served on the town council from 2000 to 2004 and worked for the sanitation department from 2004 to 2011.

EDWARD ROBINSON
FAN AND BROTHER OF DECEASED CARL "SALLY" ROBINSON

Edward was the brother of Carl "Sally" Robinson, an All-Star player in the 1970s who passed away a few years ago. His cousins Will and Anthony Robinson both played for the All-Stars as well. Will's narrative is included in this book. Edward and Carl lived in Prince Edward County, but during the school closing, they were able to be picked up by a Cumberland County school bus that took them to school in Cumberland. They were able to ride the bus for some time and attended school in Cumberland County. When neighbors found out about this deception, other children began arriving at the bus stop to catch the bus to Cumberland. Many surrounding counties were experiencing similar situations as parents tried getting their children in school.

Edward enjoyed coming to the games to watch his brother play for the All-Stars. He also enjoyed the party and family atmosphere that prevailed at each weekend game. For many of the African American players and fans, baseball was one of the few activities available in south-side Virginia during that time period.

Edward also mentioned that he loved riding his Honda Gold Wing motorcycle and felt that it rode better than a Harley-Davidson Ultra Glide. Edward said he was looking forward to the reunion to be held in September 2015.

Edward Robinson

CHUCK REID

Chuck has spent the majority of his life in Farmville/Prince Edward County. During the school closing, he did not attend school. His siblings did leave the area in order to continue their education, and he received some instruction through the various churches. He said that many students, including him, were scared and felt lost when they returned to school. The "lost children," as he described them, suffered in many ways. Being deprived of an education for five years engendered fear of failure in many Prince Edward children. Several students, Chuck included, were eventually offered college scholarships but turned them down. Many of these students felt they weren't prepared for the rigors of a college education. Promising students were just cast adrift, wanting to succeed in life but fearful that they didn't have the skills necessary to tackle college requirements and study habits.

Chuck now serves as the vice mayor of the town of Farmville and is employed by the US Post Office.

GERALD SPATES

Gerald Spates, now the town manager of Farmville, Virginia, grew up in Kensington, Maryland. He joined the army in the mid-1960s, serving in Vietnam, Fort Belvoir in Northern Virginia, and Fort Pickett in southern Virginia. After leaving the service, Gerald came to Farmville in 1973 and served on the town's planning commission. Two years later, he was appointed to run the town's government as the town manager. He's still serving in this position and has seen both the town of Farmville and Longwood University grow and prosper.

When he took over as town manager, he did a survey to find out the areas that needed renovation or major attention. Many times this meant that projects were begun to improve living conditions in African American neighborhoods. Since Gerald arrived after the schools reopened, he did not face all of the turbulence that engulfed the town and county for so many years.

Growing up in the DC area, Gerald interacted with African Americans on a regular basis. Race wasn't an issue with him, as he went to school with them and competed against them on the ball field. He met Lorenzo and Ricky and soon after began playing softball against them and other members of the All-Stars. He remembers playing in many softball leagues with the All-Stars, especially traveling to Richmond for the numerous tournaments there.

Gerald feels the racial atmosphere is good in Prince Edward County. After so many years of service to this community, he has a good idea of what transpired during the lost years and how to bring the community even closer.

Jerry Spates

Epilogue

FORTY YEARS LATER, THE REMAINING All-Stars are still a presence in their communities. From North Carolina to several cities and towns in Virginia, these individual men overcame years of oppression they encountered in Prince Edward County. They put aside their collective and individual feelings about a white man joining their team in order to find new ways to win ball games and succeed in the game of life. The spirit that saw them relish their baseball victories helped them, I feel, deal with the consequences of having no formal education for five years. They exhibited an indomitable desire to succeed… and did so in so many ways. Each is a testament to the conviction that peaceful integration can be accomplished. The Farmville All-Stars remain larger than life in their respective communities and are beacons of hope for living peacefully in a small Virginia county once fraught with hatred and despair.

As for me, I was humbled to play with such good ballplayers and such great friends. Playing for the Farmville All-Stars so many years ago fulfilled my desire to play professional baseball. As far as I'm concerned, my dream came true!

In Memoriam
Clem Jackson
Elwood Cox
Herbert Jackson
Carl Robinson
James Edward Jackson

James Robert Jackson
Garland Perkins
Robert Lewis Carter

Dad and Josh

ABOUT

Richard J. Aubry, Jr.

Richard Aubry, Ed.D., played for the Farmville All-Stars for three years in the 1970s. During that time, Richard celebrated a twenty-two-game winning streak, and was named pitcher of the year in 1976. He remains close friends with the other players.

Richard has multiple degrees from the University of Virginia. In addition to being a college professor, he has also worked as a school teacher, principal, director of instruction, and assistant superintendent. He now lives in Florida with his wife.

Ricky Brown

Coauthor Warren (Ricky) Brown was co-captain of the Farmville All Stars when Richard joined. A native of Farmville, he was the first African American to work for the Farmville Police Department who had been trained at the Police Training Center. His biggest accomplishment is persevering when the public schools closed in his community. He became a success without his father living at home.

Made in the USA
Charleston, SC
16 August 2016